TRANSFORMED BY LOVE

MEMOIR OF A SPIRITUAL JOURNEY

JAMES CALLAHAN

βίος Books
New York

βίος **Books**
An imprint of Woodwrit, Inc. Editions

TRANSFORMED BY LOVE. Copyright © 2024 by James Callahan. All rights reserved, including the right to reproduce this book or portions thereof in any form whatsoever, allowing only for brief quotations in printed reviews. Inquire at:

Woodwrit, Inc. Editions, 135 West 10th Street, ste. 11, New York, NY 10014, or email info@woodwrit.com.

ISBN: 978-1-949596-13-7

For Claire

Front Cover: Claire and Jim in front of the Heidelberg University Museum of Art, Germany 1988, commemorating the Manesse illuminated manuscript created 1300 to 1340.

CONTENTS

Part I   1
A Force of Love and Caring

Part II   43
Do You Know Jesus?

Part III   79
Transformed by Love

Part IV   107
Helpin' Han'

Part V   151
In My Inmost Being, You Teach Me Wisdom

Epilogue   189

Acknowledgments   191
Notes   193

Part 1

A Force of Love and Caring

I

"He's gone!" Claire's father, Bernie Lyons, was dead. Her brother John had just called to say that he had died at home, suddenly, of a heart attack. I held her, her voice straining with relief, anger, and grief. The demon that haunted her childhood, teenage, and even adult years was gone.

Claire often told me how, as a four-year-old, she'd tremble at the thought of her father coming home drunk. She'd squeeze herself between his living room chair and the window. Fingertips on the windowsill, she'd wait to see how much he was staggering when he passed under the streetlight. Her mother, Nellie, reading in her chair a few feet away, would say, "Look at you, you silly thing."

The "silly thing" was a child, terrified of how he would scream and threaten. Terrified that he would hit her mother, or her, again. Terrified that even her big brother Phil, a fearless five-year-old, wouldn't be able to protect them. Claire's mother was terrified too, but she couldn't admit it. She, like other battered wives of abusive, alcoholic husbands, was frozen in fear and denial.

Claire would pick up a toy and pretend to play for a few minutes. But as soon as Nellie went back to her reading, she'd creep back to the window to watch.

Bernie Lyons was mean-spirited, drunk or sober. He was cold, never gave a gift, not even to his wife and children, and expected them to absorb his cruelty without complaint. The night he fell into the Christmas tree, he made the children put it back up.

Like many abusive men, Bernie had a charming side. He was smart, and could quickly see to the heart of issues. He could organize and lead a team, and instill confidence. He had a remarkable sense of humor, and was a master of the quick retort.

He was known as the "Mayor of Danversport" (the 'Port) because of his energetic contributions to the community where Claire grew up.[1] He was admired for his bravery as a forty-year volunteer captain of the Fire Department, and as a World War I Navy veteran. He proudly led the annual Veterans' Day Parade. When Nellie married Bernie, he was president of the Pioneer Total Abstinence Association!

"Everyone in the 'Port thought he was a model of civic virtue," Claire would tell me, her cheeks flushing with anger. "They had no idea. No idea at all."

Claire's mother was a refined and intelligent woman who had graduated first in her class from Notre Dame Academy (Boston, Roxbury). She received a score of 99 on the U.S. Civil Service Examination, and could have had a bright future had she not married a man who became a raging alcoholic. Instead, she was a stay-at-home mother to five children, living vicariously through the poetry and novels she devoured. Claire was born on August 12, 1928, fifteen months after Phil; her siblings Joe, Eleanor, and John followed close behind.

The family lived at 34 River Street, a two-story house on a peninsula between the Porter and Crane rivers. Every day, Claire would watch barges unload their cargo at the Danvers River wharf, a hundred yards from the family home. Up the Porter River, near the Liberty Street bridge, more barges delivered wood to the sawmill at the Calvin Putnam Lumber Company.

The 'Port had a reputation as a rough neighborhood. Young "wharf rats," as they were called, stuck together in skirmishes with kids from "better" neighborhoods. Although Bernie drank and gambled away most of his paycheck from the Creese and Cook Tannery, and the kids had to make do with secondhand shoes and clothing from the Morgan Memorial Goodwill store, Nellie instilled in them a sense that each was precious, worthy, and loved. She taught them to read before school age, and Claire looked forward to daily walks to the library and coming home with a bag of books.

If one of the children got sick, Nellie would put a bell on the table beside the bed, so the child could ring for help.

Once, when Claire was ill, Nellie called Dr. Moriarty, crying.

"Oh, Nellie, you've had sick children before," he said.

"But this is my Claire," Nellie replied.

Claire, sitting nearby with a hot water bottle pressed to her tummy, heard something in her mother's voice that both frightened and excited her. She knew that mothers were supposed to love their children, but *this* love—almost desperate in its intensity—was special.

Claire was five when her mother's sister, Mary Margaret, died. She would find her mother sitting in her living room chair, her apron to her face, sobbing. "Please don't cry, Mama," Claire would say. "When you cry, I cry." And her mother would say, "Oh, sweet Claire, I'll try to stop crying."

With Mary's passing, Nellie lost an adult confidante with whom to talk about her troubles, which increased as the Great Depression settled over the country. She and Bernie argued constantly about money, arguments that often ended in violent scenes.

Claire and her brothers and sister schemed about how to convince their mother to leave him. Claire hoped that her grandmother or one of her uncles would help the family deal with her father's behavior. None did.

When her mother went to the parish priest, he told her to "just back him up against the wall and tell him, 'Cut it out!'"

Nellie replied, "Oh, Father, I couldn't do that."

She was right. Standing up to Bernie without support from the extended family and community would only increase his violence. Nor could Nellie tell the bars to "shut him off." If a wife with children asked, the bars would do it, but the risk of provoking further violence was high. This left Nellie trapped. Realizing that she could not get Bernie to change his behavior, she put her energy into protecting the children from his rages, while encouraging them to do well at school so they could have a better and happier future.

Claire and Phil were the first line of defense against Bernie's violence. Even as a small boy, Phil would tackle Bernie when he was abusing their mother, while Claire would ensure the younger children stayed hidden away. At night, when her brother John was terrified, she would hear a soft knock on her bedroom door. "Clay, Clay, are you awake?" She'd let him in, and they would talk, until he fell asleep.

2

The suffering that Claire and her siblings experienced at home was tempered by the joy they felt in visits to Nana Mahoney (her maternal grandmother) and the uncles and aunts at their family home at 91 Anawan Avenue in Boston. Nana was a warm and generous woman who loved to tease the grandchildren by asking, "Who am I?" The children would reply, "Nana Mahoney!" And she'd say, "I'm Ellen Kilty Sullivan Mahoney from Ireland, County Cork, Bantry Bay, Schull, Garranes."

She would tell them stories of Ireland, and how her grandfather had seen the French fleet off Bantry Bay,[1] and of the snobbery that existed when the family immigrated to Boston, where signs in store windows read, "No Irish Need Apply." Claire would listen wide-eyed. Why couldn't she live *here*, in this book-filled house where a pot of tea was always steeping on the antique table, and where those in the family were always speaking of art, history, music, and news? Why did they always have to go home to Bernie's violence?

Claire's great-aunts, Harriet (Hattie) and Lucy Sullivan, owned a dressmaker's shop on Chambers Street in Boston's

West End, an airy, perfume-smelling place Claire was fond of visiting. Her aunt Annie Sullivan, in Manhattan, was a glamorous and stately widow with three small girls: Claire's cousins Midge, Ellen, and Ann.

Her aunt Mary Margaret was society editor for the *Boston American*.[2] She loved to regale Claire with stories of balls she attended, and about the ladies' elegant dresses, the handsome men, the music, and the flowers.

She once showed Claire a box of newspaper clippings.

"Look, Claire," she said, "I write these articles, and everyone in Boston reads them!"

These Mahoney women were models for Claire's sense of sophistication, adventure, and independence. Later in life, it would pain Claire to think that, although Nellie shared her sisters' and aunts' intelligence and drive, she had never gotten to live the kind of rich and stimulating life they enjoyed.

Claire's uncle Joe Mahoney was a graduate of the Boston Latin School, and, in 1915, from Boston College. A reader with an extensive library, Joe was about five-foot-nine with a thin, pale face, wispy hair, a long, pointed nose, a gravelly voice, a grand sense of humor, and a soft, high-pitched laugh. Warm and gentle, he loved to hug. He smoked, and enjoyed Jameson Irish Whiskey. When he had a complaint about a company's faulty product he would send the company a postcard, so that everyone who handled the card along the way could read about it!

Joe and his brother John taught high school in the Boston school system. Though he was offered a position at Boston Latin—the oldest school in America and the most prestigious high school in Boston—Joe chose to teach English and history in a high school for underprivileged students. Joe's choice to serve the underprivileged made an impression on Claire, whose own inclination toward service was already forming.

When Mary Margaret passed away, the Anawan Avenue home became too expensive to manage. Joe, John, and Nana Mahoney moved to a first-floor apartment on the corner of Huntington and Hemenway, a block from the Boston Museum of Fine Arts. Claire spent happy hours as a child wandering the exhibits with Uncle Joe, and was particularly entranced by the Egyptian collection. Joe also took her to bookstores, to the Harvard Coop, and to school to watch him teach.

Claire's uncle John was loving too, if less approachable than Joe. On his days off, he enjoyed lounging in his smoking jacket and reading the *New York Times* and *Boston Globe*. On one occasion, when Claire was about five, he spoke to her sharply. She surprised him by announcing, "I'm going home to my father, but I'll be back, boy." She left the house and started down the street, hoping he or Uncle Joe would bring her back, because she had no idea how to get to Danvers. Joe ran to get her, enveloping her in the safety and care she needed so badly.

On her father's side, Claire had one uncle and no aunts. Her uncle Joe Lyons lived in Manhattan. He never married, had no children, and was, like Bernie, an alcoholic. Unlike Bernie, he was kind and never failed to take the children to Mrs. Cahill's candy store. Once, at Thanksgiving dinner, one of her brothers asked Bernie, "May I have more turkey, please?" Bernie said, "You've had enough." Uncle Joe Lyons came to the boy's defense. "Bernie, it's Thanksgiving. Give the children more turkey!"

The next day, when Claire saw her uncle preparing to leave, his car at the curb, she ran upstairs, threw some panties in a suitcase, and came running back down, the suitcase bumping on the stairs behind her. "Uncle Joe, Uncle Joe," she called, "I want to go with you." He sat on the porch step, took her on his lap, and tried to explain why she couldn't go. She sobbed and sobbed. He held her and kissed her on the forehead, saying, "My dearest Claire, I'll come back; I'll come back." She stopped crying. He drove away. Several months later he died when his car collided with a train.

Claire resented that she had to live with Bernie and his violence; that no one came to take her and her siblings away. Why *not* live with the Mahoneys? Yet even at five it was becoming clear that although many people loved her, nobody was coming to rescue her. They could only lend her the strength she needed to find a way out on her own.

3

In the absence of protection from the adults, Claire and her siblings formed tight bonds with each other. Claire's first friend was Phil. A robust boy, he was as full of bravado and aggression as Claire was retiring and reticent. She said, "Phil was a wild man." When they discussed Bernie's violence, Phil would declare, "I'm not afraid of him!" To which Claire would reply, "I am!"

Wild man or not, Claire enjoyed their exploits. Claire was five, Phil six, when they rode the train, unaccompanied, from Danversport to Boston to see Gene Autry, the "Singing Cowboy" of films and radio. Even in 1933 that was a bit daring for two little children. Their presence on the train raised eyebrows, but Claire and Phil were unruffled. At Boston Garden, they wove their way between a sea of adult legs until they reached the edge of the stage. There he was—their cowboy, crooning "The Yellow Rose of Texas" and strumming his guitar. *Maybe he'll let us ride back to Texas with him on his horse*, Claire thought. *Or get us into the movies, and we'll never have to go home again.*

Two years later, they took the train to Canobie Lake Park in Salem, New Hampshire, where they were among the first to ride the Yankee Cannonball. When she saw the ride's steep drops and veering turns, Claire felt queasy. "Phil, it's too scary," she said. "I don't want to get on."

"You'd better get on," Phil said, "or I won't give you the money for the train ride home. You'll be stuck here all night, and you'll have to sleep under the merry-go-round."

As they were standing in line, Claire saw a Danvers neighbor boy being helped off the ride, his face pale and his legs shaky.

"Phil," she said, "I really don't want to do it!"

"Don't be a baby, Claire. Just think how jealous everyone at school is going to be."

When they got to the front of the line and an empty car clicked into place, Claire thought she would cry. Still, she took Phil's hand and climbed in.

As soon as the car started moving, she slid under her lap restraint and lay on the floor with her eyes squeezed shut. Meanwhile, Phil roared with excitement each time the Cannonball whizzed around a turn, his hair blowing in the wind.

When they got home, Phil boasted about the fearless way they'd tamed the Cannonball while other kids chickened out. Claire kept quiet, hoping she would never have to do it again.

The next big adventure came in June 1938, when President Roosevelt stopped in Salem while in Massachusetts for his son's wedding in Nahant. An officer of the American Federation of Labor, Bernie had been a supporter of Roosevelt and the New Deal. But he left the Democratic Party when the president tried to pack the Supreme Court in 1937.

Regardless of his political feelings, he knew it would be exciting for his children to see the president—a rare moment of thoughtfulness on Bernie's part, although Claire would later wonder if he was motivated more by a desire to boast of this occasion to his friends than by a genuine interest in his children's happiness. They took the train to Salem to see the president.

A Secret Service agent saw them pushing their way to the front of the crowd. He took them by the hand and said, "Come up here, kids. Stand with me. His car is going to have to stop to open the gate, and you can get right next to it."

When the open-top limousine stopped, Phil and Claire were three feet from the president. He gave them a wide smile, his signature cigarette holder clamped between his teeth. Decades later, she still remembered that warm summer day, the gleaming black limousine, and the smell of tobacco on President Roosevelt's breath.

Meeting President Roosevelt was a bright spot in a year of worsening violence at home. Although she no longer waited by the living room window to see how badly he was staggering, Claire still lived in dread of Bernie's nightly return from the bar, and the havoc that inevitably ensued. Her mother's refusal to leave Bernie, and the failure of the parish priest or other adult to intervene on Nellie's and the children's behalf, made her feel hopeless.

This might have crushed Claire's spirit if not for her fifth-grade teacher, Sr. Margaret Saint Paul Cawley. Claire had transferred to Saint Mary, Star of the Sea elementary school in Beverly after attending the 'Port school for grades one through four. A gregarious woman with warm blue eyes, Sr. Margaret welcomed Claire and made sure the other children included her in their games. "My, you're good at spelling," she'd say. "Maybe you'll be a teacher someday."

Claire soaked up her encouragement. She woke up every morning eager to go to school and impress Sr. Margaret with how well she'd completed the latest assignment.

One morning, Sr. Margaret announced that the first student to memorize the Beatitudes would win a holy card.[1] "I'll award the prize right after recess," she said. As soon as the bell rang, Claire made her way to Sr. Margaret's desk. "Can I recite the Beatitudes now?" she said. When she'd finished, Sr. Margaret said, "That's wonderful. But Claire, when did you memorize them?"

"During arithmetic," Claire said proudly.

Sr. Margaret tried her best to look stern. "Claire," she said, "you should have been paying attention to the arithmetic lesson."

Seeing Claire's face fall, she swiftly added, "I'm still going to give you the prize, because you *did* memorize the Beatitudes. But I'm also going to give a prize to the student who memorized them during recess."

Sure enough, when recess was over, Sr. Margaret awarded a second holy card to another student. But Claire knew that she was the first!

4

In the summers, the children's focus shifted from school to Sandy Beach Park, a pleasant and popular spot on the Porter River fifty yards from the family's back door. The playground instructor, Joe Halupowski, was always coming up with activities for the children, or teaching them popular dance steps, like the Virginia Reel.

But the highlight of the summer was the annual running competition. Even though as a child and through her teens Claire suffered from painful leg cramps, she was a natural-born runner. The summer she turned twelve, she won every race in her age group. She was buoyant with elation, her brow still tinged with sweat and her chest bright with first-place ribbons, when the organizers took her aside.

"Next year," they told her, "we're only going to let you enter one race. It's just not fair to the other kids."

Although another child might have been outraged at this injustice, Claire was undaunted. "That's fine," she said. "Just tell me which race has the best prize!"

Claire's physical vigor was matched by an inner strength and conviction that began to take shape as she grew into a teen. When Claire was in high school, she became her siblings' spokesperson in the ongoing campaign to convince Nellie to leave Bernie.

"Go stay with Nana Mahoney," Claire would urge Nellie the morning after a drunken scene. "Take the train now, while he's at work. The boys are big enough to deal with him, and I can cook and run the house while you're gone."

"Oh, I don't know," Nellie would demur, busying herself with the dishes. "You kids mind your own business."

But one day in 1946, she surprised Claire by agreeing to the plan.

The day before Nellie left, Claire called Phil, who was a patient at the Chelsea Naval Hospital, to tell him what was to happen. He got a two-day pass, and was waiting at 34 River Street when their father came home from work.

When Bernie walked in the door, Phil said, "Well, she finally left you." Claire was standing at the stove, cooking the evening meal. Bernie grabbed her arm to turn her to face him. "Is that true?" he said.

"Take your hand off me," Claire said. "I'm not your wife."

There was much, *much* more Claire wanted to say—years of suppressed rage at the way his selfishness and violence had cast a shadow over the lives of everyone close to him. But even by this single utterance of contempt, in defense of her mother and siblings, Claire touched a strength in herself she didn't know she had.

The next evening, Claire listened as Bernie called Nellie on the phone and promised that he had stopped drinking for good—a claim that set Claire's teeth on edge. She could barely make out her mother's responses coming through the receiver.

A FORCE OF LOVE AND CARING

"I'll come home in two weeks, Bernie," Nellie said. "But if you start drinking again, I'm going to leave for good."

Claire felt a surge of pride at hearing her mother's words, but it was swiftly followed by worry. Would Nellie follow through on this ultimatum? Or would she find yet another excuse and come home?

For the next two weeks, Bernie came straight home from work and ate the meals Claire grudgingly served him. On the last day, Nellie came home.

"He's only going to start drinking again," Claire told her. "You should have stayed away longer."

"I told him two weeks, and I'm keeping my word," Nellie replied.

It wasn't long before Bernie started coming home drunk.

"Now will you leave him for good?" Claire said the next time she got her mother alone. "You promised you would."

"Oh Claire, I can't do that," Nellie said.

This refusal angered Claire. She'd drawn on deep inner reserves to orchestrate this intervention, only to see the gains slipping away.

"You're losing everything we fought for," she said, her voice thickening with tears. "If the six of us were lined up against that wall and you had to make a choice, you'd choose him."

"Bold thing," said Nellie.

In anger, Claire answered, "It's *true*."

A few months later, Nana Mahoney died, leaving Claire bereft of a warm and loving mentor, and Nellie of a potential haven. *Now Mama's never going to leave him*, Claire thought.

She stopped urging Nellie to leave, and instead put her energy into poring over college catalogs, dreaming of the day that she, Claire, could finally leave the family home. Thanks to Bernie's drinking and gambling, her family couldn't afford the tuition. They couldn't even afford Phil's final semester of high school at St. John's Prep, and Claire had been outraged when the religious brothers kicked him out just months before graduation, an injustice she would remember for the rest of her life.

When she graduated from high school, Claire enrolled in the Fay School, a one-year secretarial school on Boston's Beacon Hill. *Executive secretaries make good money*, Claire thought. *I can work a few years and save for college.*

Shortly after graduating from Fay, she found a job with a Salem attorney.

Just when she'd finally gained some independence, her mother surprised everyone by telling Bernie she was going to leave him if he didn't stop drinking—and Bernie surprised everyone by quitting for good.

Claire's pride in and happiness for her mother was mixed with anguish. Why had Nellie finally found the strength *now*, when the damage was already done? *We needed her to leave when we were kids*, Claire thought. *What good does it do us now that we're grown?*

She could barely contain her resentment when Bernie started attending AA meetings, and preaching the virtues of sobriety to anyone who would listen. "Funny thing," she told me once, "he never completed Step Nine, to make 'direct amends' to all persons he had harmed.[1] Make amends! He never even told us he was sorry."

Phil, Joe, Eleanor, and John struggled with alcoholism throughout their lives, with devastating consequences for them, their marriages, their children, and their careers. Only Claire escaped the suffering of excessive alcohol use. She devoted much of her professional life to helping those caught in the grip of what she came to understand is a family disease.

5

Claire had dated in high school and while at the Fay School, and dreamed of someday getting married and becoming a mother. But at the same time, she'd begun to feel a quiet tug toward the Church.

In the summer of 1950, she attended a retreat at Holy Cross Academy in Brookline, an affluent suburb south of Boston. After a few days praying and strolling the grounds, she took one of the Holy Cross nuns aside.

"Tell me the hardest thing about being a nun," Claire said, "and if I know I can do that, then I know I can be a nun."

Decades later, Claire could not remember what the nun replied—but it must have confirmed something for her. At the end of the retreat, she asked the Sisters of the Holy Cross to allow her to enter the postulancy, a one-year program during which she would live as a sister, and enroll as a college freshman at Saint Mary's College, Notre Dame, Indiana.

A week or two after the retreat, she went out for lunch with her high school best friend, Patsy Kelaher. It was a sunny day, and the two girls chatted about music and books for nearly an hour before Claire said, "Patsy, I've decided to go into the convent."

Patsy was shocked. "No, you're not!" she exclaimed, nearly spilling her coffee.

Claire opened her shopping bag and silently pulled out a pair of long, black stockings. "Oh my God, Claire," Patsy said, and began to cry. "What about getting married? Having kids? That's what you've always wanted!"

"I know," Claire said. "I've thought about this long and hard. I *do* want those things. But I want this more."

The reaction at home was no less surprised. Nellie was warmly encouraging of her daughter's decision. This would give Claire access to higher education, and save her from getting married young and ending up in a similar position to Nellie. As for Bernie, he was over the moon. A nun or priest in the family was a source of pride for Irish Catholics, and he wasted no time in letting everyone know that *his daughter* was devoting her life to the Church. *He'd* raised her right!

The Sisters of the Holy Cross approved Claire's request, and on a warm Sunday in September, the family went to Boston to attend Claire's departure ceremony. Claire had butterflies in her stomach all morning, and cried a little when Boston Archbishop Cardinal Cushing delivered his homily. The next day, she took the train to South Bend to enter the postulancy—the first step toward becoming a nun.

The convent was located on a bluff overlooking the Saint Joseph River, set amid castle-like stone buildings and sycamore, maple, and oak trees. It was the furthest Claire had been from home. Her days flowed by in a routine of attendance at Mass, classes, study, assisting the nuns with various tasks, eating meals in community, praying, and meditating. As she strolled the beautiful grounds, she marveled at her happiness. *This is exactly how I want to live,* she thought. *I'm so grateful to God for calling me here.*

At the end of her eleven-month postulancy, Claire eagerly agreed to remain at the convent and receive the habit—marking an official transition from secular to religious life. She had no doubt that she wanted to continue on this path. Here she was, attending university, praying, living in community, and feeling closer to God.

When she received the habit, Claire also received a new name. As the day of the ceremony approached, she heard that the sisters might assign her the name Sr. Mary Helen Bernard as a way of drawing her parents closer in their marriage—casting an unexpected shadow on a happy day. Distressed, she went to Sr. Marianna Heppen, the assistant director of Postulants and Novices, and said, "I hope they don't do that. I don't want those names." Yet on the day of the naming ceremony, they named her Sr. Helen Bernard.

Afterward, as the nuns mingled in the courtyard, Sr. Marianna asked how she liked her new name. "I don't like it any more today than I did yesterday," Claire replied. She knew the sisters may have had good intentions, but it made her angry that they hadn't bothered to ask her why she objected so strongly. The reason was that she did not wish to be constantly reminded of her parents' painful marriage, and the suffering in the home. But now she would think of it every time someone spoke her name.

Claire spent three more happy years in South Bend, working toward her bachelor's degree, and, in August 1953, made her profession of "temporary" vows of poverty, chastity, and obedience. By vowing to live a life of poverty, she agreed to share any income or gifts with her religious community. By vowing to be obedient, she agreed to abide by the decisions of her superiors. By vowing to be celibate, she agreed to give up not only marriage and children, but the unique love and intimacy these represented.

Claire spent her fourth year as a student sixth-grade teacher at the Laboratory School, Saint Mary's College. It was an easy assignment. Students came from three affluent South Bend parishes, or were children of Saint Mary's and Notre Dame faculty. Small class sizes made them manageable. Although Claire looked forward to serving the underprivileged like her uncle Joe, the Laboratory School was a good place to test her skills under the supervision of an experienced teacher.

On one occasion, Claire was asked to substitute for a first-grade teacher. While briefing her, the teacher said, "When you take them to the bathroom, tell them 'Now make sure you go to the bathroom on this visit, because we won't be coming back this morning.'" Sure enough, shortly after the bathroom visit, a little girl raised her hand.

"Sister," she said, "I have to go to the bathroom real bad, and if you let me go just this one time, I'll never go again the rest of my life." Claire said, "Sweetheart, you can go now, and you can go as often as you want for the rest of your life."

6

In the summer of 1954, the Sisters of the Holy Cross gave Claire a two-year assignment to teach at Blessed Sacrament School, in Chevy Chase, Maryland, near the Maryland/D.C. line. In the 1950s, Washington, D.C. was racially segregated. As a Northerner, Claire had never seen separate water fountains for whites and blacks, or signs indicating separate seating areas at diners and restaurants.

She was relieved to find that, although it was in an affluent neighborhood and attended by the children of ambassadors and high-ranking government officials, Blessed Sacrament was *not* segregated. *Just imagine writing to Uncle Joe Mahoney,* she thought, *and telling him I'm teaching at a wealthy, elite, upper-class school that doesn't admit black children!*

One of her extracurricular duties was to oversee the training and conduct of the student "crossing guards" responsible for stopping traffic to allow the children to safely cross the intersections. One of her students, an avid guard, was the son of the dean of the Corps of Foreign Diplomates, Guillermo Sevilla Sacasa.[1]

Though named Guillermo after his father, his classmates used the English nickname for William, calling him "Willy

A FORCE OF LOVE AND CARING

Sevilly." His father had been a judge and leader of the Nicaraguan National Assembly, and was known as the "world's most decorated ambassador," having received fifty international decorations and accumulated hundreds of photographs with visiting dignitaries and U.S. presidents. But to "Willy Sevilly," his white crossing guard belt was the equal of his father's many decorations. He wore his belt with pride!

AT THE END of her two years at Blessed Sacrament, Claire made her "final" vows of poverty, chastity, and obedience. She was twenty-eight. A few days later, she traveled by train to her new assignment: to teach eighth grade at Saint Paul the Apostle School, in Hell's Kitchen, Manhattan.

In those days, Hell's Kitchen was a tenement neighborhood of mostly poor and working-class Irish, Puerto Rican, Italian, Polish, and Greek families. The fifty-five eighth-graders she'd be teaching were the children of longshoremen, factory workers, waitresses—a far cry from the diplomats' children in Chevy Chase. Their parents worked nights, and some of them belonged to the Irish gangs that controlled the neighborhood. Crime and domestic violence were high.[2]

When Claire asked one boy if he was afraid to sleep alone when his parents were working nights, he said, "Oh, no, Sister, I have the butcher knife right beside me in bed." When she asked another why he was falling asleep in class, he said, "My mother told me to sleep in the hall again last night, because she and my father were fighting." When the same boy was late in returning from lunch recess, and Claire asked him why, he said,

"They were putting all our furniture out on the street, and I had to help move it." "Oh, that's all right that you're late," she said, scarcely holding back tears.

Uncle Joe Mahoney cheered when he learned Claire was finally teaching poor children. When she described her students, he told her they reminded him of the children he taught in the technical high school in Boston. She was proud of carrying on Uncle Joe's legacy, and determined to bring the best of her talents to serve these bright but underprivileged young people.

Still, it was a steep learning curve. When she sent a note home with a boy's report card, as was the custom at Blessed Sacrament, she learned that you don't do that at Saint Paul's. The student came back the next morning with black eyes and a bruised face.

Claire more than made up for the occasional misstep with her fierce dedication to the students. When one of them told her that other kids in the school said they were the dumb class, Claire looked him straight in the eye and deadpanned: "I don't teach dummies."

When a girl who was going to have Claire as her eighth-grade teacher asked one of Claire's students what she was like, the friend answered, "She's tough, but she fights for you."

To make sure her students graduated and could compete for good high schools, she offered to tutor them every morning for an hour before school started. She wasn't expecting many to take her offer. But when she opened the school door on the first morning of this special class, she saw a long line of children, some with torn or threadbare sweaters, standing in the cold. The children's eagerness to learn reminded Claire of her own enthusiasm to go to school, no matter how dire things got at home.

As eager as she was to continue at Saint Paul's, it was not in Claire's power to remain at the school. In 1958, the Sisters of the Holy Cross transferred her from Saint Paul's to Saint Mary's Academy high school in Alexandria, Virginia. When the cab showed up to take her to the train station, her students lined the street to wave goodbye. She cried, wondering how they would make it without her—*if* they would make it without her. She often spoke to me about those kids, describing them with such love that it felt like they were in our living room.

WHEN CLAIRE'S CAB pulled up to the curb on Russell Road in Alexandria, she saw six nuns in rocking chairs on the convent porch. A seventh chair was vacant. Claire thought, *Oh, my God, that empty chair is for me!* She was thirty, the youngest of the thirteen nuns at the Academy.

Alexandria, Virginia could not be more different from Hell's Kitchen. Set along the Potomac River, the town had a stately feel. Hell's Kitchen was cramped and noisy; Alexandria was spacious and clean, with fresh air. Though many of the girls were from affluent or relatively affluent families, Claire knew that they, like the children she had taught at Blessed Sacrament and Saint Paul's, were seeking their way in life. She knew that helping them find their way would be just as important as giving them a grounding in history, government, and religion.

There were advantages to teaching government studies across the Potomac from Washington—not to mention being a religious sister from Massachusetts at a time when John F. Kennedy was in the Senate and soon to be president. When Claire called Senator Kennedy's office to request House of Representatives' gallery seat tickets for her and her students to attend the opening session of Congress, the tickets were couriered to the school the next day.

Advantages of teaching in the nation's capital were also apparent when, in the U.S. history course, the class discussion turned to the question of the Soviet/U.S. Missile Gap. After a long back-and-forth, a student raised her hand and said, "Well, General Twining was our guest at dinner last night, and he said, 'There is no missile gap; the U.S has superiority in that regard.'"3

FOR THE SUMMER OF 1962, Claire worked at Saint Joseph's Home and School for Boys in Washington, D.C. One Sunday afternoon, an eight-year-old boy was waiting for his mother. "My mother is working," he told Claire, "but she's coming to see me when she gets off."

Claire waited with the boy all afternoon, playing ping-pong and making up games to keep him occupied throughout the long hours. They waited past supper and into early evening, the boy growing restless, Claire doing her best to soothe him. When night fell and it was apparent his mother wasn't going to come, the boy lashed out at Claire, striking her with his fists, and shouting, "I hate you, I hate you, I hate you!"

All Claire could do was hold the boy and try to comfort him as he expressed his rage and frustration. Later, she learned that his mother was a prostitute who had placed him at Saint Joseph's because she couldn't care for him. In moments like these, Claire felt her heart would break. What would become of this child? Where would he find love in his life? Could he ever understand the love she felt for him in that moment, even as she was the closest available target for his grief?

7

That fall, Claire received a new teaching assignment at Saint Mary's Academy high school in Austin, Texas. The year 1962 was a turbulent time to be a Catholic—especially a Catholic nun. The Vatican II Council opened in October. She followed the proceedings with interest, devouring articles and discussions about the "universal call to holiness," which was now being set forward by the Church.[1] While Catholic teaching had traditionally presented the religious life of nuns and priests as a "higher" calling, the Church was now saying that these vocations were on an equal footing with all other ways of serving God and the community.

For some sisters, brothers, and priests, Vatican II bolstered their commitment to their religious vows. Others saw the "universal call to holiness" as a call to reassess their lives and choose new forms of dedication to God. If one could serve God equally well as a married layperson, why put up with the intrusive and controlling bureaucracy associated with being a nun or brother?

These were questions Claire was asking, especially as she chafed under the supervision of her new principal and religious superior, Sr. Rose Anthony. Claire was stunned when Rose Anthony informed her that she would be teaching French.

"French?" Claire replied. "If I am to make a contribution, I should be teaching in my field, history and government."

"You'll make a contribution by doing what you're told!" Rose Anthony rebutted.

Claire was shocked by her rudeness, and the arbitrariness of the decision grated on her. Was this how Claire was going to spend the rest of her life, shuffled from assignment to assignment, subjected to the whims of superiors like Rose Anthony, who could use her position to force compliance with her will, and squander Claire's and others' talents and education?

Claire learned from other sisters that she was not the only one who had felt the pain of Rose Anthony's demeaning treatment. Sr. Miriam Francis had left the convent following a nasty encounter with her. The following year, Rose Anthony was riding Sr. Denita especially hard, criticizing her relentlessly. It reached a point where Sr. Ellenice went into what she called "a red rage." She confronted Rose Anthony, shouting, "Ease up on her, or you'll drive her out, just as you drove out Miriam Francis."

Claire was in the room when this scene took place, her stomach in knots. Shouting at one's superior was not done! At the same time, she was grateful to Sr. Ellenice for having the courage to say what everyone else was thinking. In other places of employment, people had the right to confront overreaching bosses. Belonging to a religious order shouldn't prevent the women from speaking up when their working conditions were intolerable. Yet as nuns, it often seemed like Claire and the other sisters didn't have the same rights they would enjoy in the secular world.

The sisters contended with Rose Anthony until Mother Loretto Conway, provincial of the Eastern Province, visited the school. The Holy Cross Constitution required biannual visits to each school, hospital, or other foundation the sisters operated. The purpose was to speak with each sister to determine how she was doing, and see if she had any special needs. The visit also looked into the administrative and financial functioning of the institution.

On the morning of Claire's meeting with Mother Loretto, rain streaked the windows of the small, sparsely furnished office on the convent's first floor.

"Sr. Helen Bernard," said Mother Loretto, two cups of tea steaming on the table between them, "the Provincial Council has been discussing the idea of sending you back to school to get your Ph.D.—after which you could join the faculty teaching at Saint Mary's College. What do you think of that?"

Claire was stunned. It was quite the offer for a Danvers girl who had once pored over the catalogs of colleges she couldn't afford, dreaming of attending even one semester of university.

A Ph.D.? she thought. *How can I turn that down?*

But over the past few months, her doubts about continuing her life as a nun had become more pressing.

"I don't know," she said carefully. "I'd love to get my Ph.D., of course. But to tell you the truth, I've been thinking about leaving the community."

Claire braced herself for a torrent of judgment or even anger, but Mother Loretto leaned in kindly, her brown eyes conveying sympathy and understanding. "No matter what you decide, you can count on my support," she said. "In the meantime, is there anything I can do for you?"

"Yes," Claire said, grateful for the kindness of this response, "there is one thing you can do for all of us here at the school."

"What is that?"

"Tell Rose Anthony to take the screws off!"

Mother Loretto's eyes widened, and Claire hoped she hadn't been too flippant. But then the provincial superior smiled.

"Thank you for letting me know," she said. "I will."

At the end of the term, Rose Anthony was transferred from the convent, and Sr. Helen Miriam (Ruth Reed) was named principal and superior. She ran the school and convent in an open and democratic way—giving Claire space to ponder her decision about remaining in the community. Claire and Ruth became fast friends.

As Claire was engaging in an internal debate about the merits and drawbacks of remaining a nun, she also made space for debate and discussion in her teaching—particularly in her religion class. It wasn't lecture and Q&A. It was: "Put your chairs in a circle, girls, and let's talk about what our faith means in our day-to-day lives."

She encouraged the girls to talk about how they treated one another; what was happening in the school that needed to be put right; about their dating habits. She encouraged them to read and react to news and current events. She led them through debates for and against the existence of God.

She emphasized the importance of individual conscience as the final arbiter of one's decisions. Looking intently at each student, she'd say, "Always remember, girls, your conscience is your guide—but you must also strive to *form* that conscience."

One hot, sunny day toward the end of the semester, she irreverently threw her cape up on her shoulders, exposing her bare arms—an unusual move, on which, years later, one student commented: "I see that as a visual metaphor for her openness to us as her students. She bared herself to us, her feelings and her ideas, and invited us to be open with her. What a beautiful woman. She was sunshine to us girls."

Claire's openness and willingness to wade into uncomfortable waters meant that the girls sought her out as a mentor and confidante. In private meetings in her office they told her about their drinking, or their parents' drinking; about domestic violence, sexual abuse, and other difficult matters.

One night, a student and her younger sister came to the convent in tears. Claire invited them in and sat with them on one of the convent's cozy brown couches.

"What's going on?" she said.

"Our mom and dad are drinking again," said the older girl, "and they started throwing things and hitting each other. Dad broke the big mirror in the living room, and it shattered everywhere."

As Claire listened, she was transported back to her own childhood. She wasn't looking at her student and her sister anymore, but at a younger version of herself and her sister Eleanor.

Claire held the girls close.

"I'm so sorry, girls," she said.

"Will you talk to our parents?" her student asked.

"I'll come to your house in the morning," Claire promised, remembering the countless times she'd wished that someone, anyone, would intervene on Bernie's violence.

She explained to the girls what she might say to their parents and asked if they would be willing to tell them, in the safety of her presence, how the drinking and violence terrorized them. They agreed. As they left, she hugged them and assured them she would do all she could to help.

The next day, Claire, dressed in her severe black habit, and grateful for the moral authority it lent her, drove to the girls' house. When she knocked on the door, the parents invited her in. Although someone had cleaned up after the previous night's fracas, there were still shards of broken mirror on the floor.

"Your girls came to see me last night," she explained, "and they asked me to speak with you. I'd like them to join us in the living room for a family conversation, if that is all right with you."

The girls timidly came out of their rooms, and when all five of them had gathered in the living room, Claire began to speak.

As though speaking of a family she knew well, but, in fact, drawing on the memories of her own childhood experience, she described nights of drunken rage, and how the children trembled and cried. How they longed to run away, to be somewhere safe—away from the drunken father.

She told the girls' parents how they were damaging their helpless girls; that their daughters may grow to hate them, rather than love them.

She turned to the two children. "Girls," she said, "can you please tell your parents how their drinking hurts you?"

Through tears, the two girls described what their parents said and did to each other and to them when they were drunk. The parents listened shame-faced, holding back tears.

A few months later, the girls' parents began to attend AA meetings—first sporadically, then with greater commitment. They drank less frequently, and eventually became sober.

Claire had managed to do for the girls what nobody had done for her—intervene on the adults who were ruining their lives. After Claire passed away, her former student wrote to me, *Claire came into my life with a force of love and caring. I will love Claire throughout eternity. She touched my very soul.*

8

One day in May 1964, Claire was walking through the Student Union at the University of Texas (UT), when she spotted a bright yellow notice stapled to a bulletin board. Walking closer, she read that the U.S. Department of State's Fulbright Commission was accepting applications for high school and university history faculty for summer 1965 awards to study abroad. Claire's pulse quickened when she saw the application deadline: two weeks away.

Although Claire was always on the lookout for opportunities for others, it was the first time in ages she had spotted one for herself. Walking home to the convent, she felt electrified with possibility.

The application inquired about her educational background, teaching experience, the aspects of world and European history she wished to study, and the countries in which she preferred to study. She named Egypt, Greece, and France.

Two months later, she received notice that she was a finalist. In October, she traveled to San Antonio to meet with a Fulbright panel of university faculty with expertise in world and European history. Then came the long months of waiting.

After a day of teaching, toward the end of March, she found a U.S. Department of State envelope on her desk at the convent. "We are pleased to announce . . . ." She quickly scanned down the page: "Institut d'Etudes Politiques, Sorbonne, Paris, France." Her heart soared.

Claire ran next door.

"Sr. Ellenice!" she exclaimed. "I'm going to *Paris!*"

They both ran down the hall, their faces bursting with smiles, to tell Sr. Denita. "I've never been out of the country before," Claire said. "I've never even been to Canada. And now I'm going to France!"

Two weeks later, a Sunday *Austin American Statesman* article read:

"Join the convent and see the world." That's how things are working out for Sister Helen Bernard, C.S.C., who is brimming with smiles over winning a Fulbright grant. The State Department made this official only a few days ago, and both Sister Helen Bernard's students and the winner herself have been walking on a happy cloud ever since. In fact, the students were so proud of their teacher that they sent a big bouquet of flowers to her the night of the announcement.[1]

In consideration of Claire's wish to attend daily Mass, the State Department made accommodations for her at the Hotel Recamier, adjacent to the church of Saint-Sulpice—the second-largest church in Paris.

Claire would never forget her first morning waking up to the sound of pigeons cooing on the cobblestoned streets below her window, or the taste of the croissant and *café au lait* the hotel's proprietor sent up to her room.

With this comfortable hotel as a base, Claire attended lectures by internationally known scholars, traveled to historic sites and monuments in France, Germany, and Italy, and took part in local and national celebrations on the anniversaries of historic events.

One memorable incident took place on Bastille Day (July 14). Most of the Hotel Recamier guests had left for the celebrations. Claire was getting a late start. In those days, there were no private bathrooms—one had to walk down the hall to take a bath. Claire donned her robe and threw a towel over her arm, only to find the bathroom door locked. She called the desk to ask if someone could bring the key. It was a small, family-managed hotel, and Claire had had friendly interactions with the husband and wife. This morning, however, she didn't recognize the voice on the phone.

"Oui, madame; tout de suite!" said a young clerk. She heard his footsteps on the stairs as he hurried up. When he turned the corner at the top of the stairs, he paused, looked Claire over, and announced, "Très jolie!" He offered his services as a personal bath attendant, but Claire took the key with a prim, "Merci."

When, dressed in her nun's garb, she passed him at the front desk on her way out, he blushed from ear to ear, forehead to chin!

Away from the daily routine of convent life, and engaged with the dynamic Fulbright faculty and other scholars, she began to envision a future outside the rigid routine of the convent.

Fulbright travels took her to Rome where her cousin, Ellen Sullivan, religion editor for *Newsweek* magazine, was covering the Vatican II Council.

"Don't be afraid to move in new directions, Claire," Ellen said. "You're only thirty-seven. If you want, you can still get married and have a family."

Claire only smiled, feeling the possibilities dance inside her like butterflies.

ON HER RETURN FROM FRANCE, she continued to teach history and government, but her interest had shifted to psychology. She had been guidance counselor at the Academy for the past year, and she decided to enroll in two psychology courses at UT, one on individual counseling, one on group counseling. Earl Koile, author of *Listening as a Way of Becoming* and *Your Secret Self,* [2] taught both courses.

Koile's person-centered approach to teaching and therapy appealed to Claire. This school of therapy, developed by psychologist Carl Rogers in the 1940s and 1950s, rejects the idea of therapists as authorities on their clients' inner experiences.[3] Instead, the therapist helps create a trusting environment in which the individual feels free to become the person he or she wants to be. Central to this process is the concept of "unconditional positive regard." By projecting an attitude of warm acceptance, the therapist makes it safe for the client to reveal and accept his or her deepest fears and most vulnerable feelings.

Claire had experienced unconditional positive regard in her relationships with Nana Mahoney and Sr. Margaret Saint Paul. She knew the power of empathy, caring and active listening to transform even the bleakest situation into something bearable or growth-enhancing.

Her interest in psychology grew, and Earl became her friend and mentor. Although only eleven years older than

Claire, she saw him as a father figure—wise, confident, and calmly encouraging of her talents.

As a Christian and religious sister, she was committed to living the commandment, "You shall love your neighbor as yourself."[4] She saw her graduate studies in psychology as a way of furthering this commitment. The person-centered approach offered a way of loving that placed Claire and her "neighbor" in sacred relationship. By listening deeply to students, and friends, she showed them a level of respect and attention that many of them had never received.

When Claire came into my life, I experienced the force of her loving attention. When I would tell her about a problem I was having at work or with a colleague or friend, she paid close attention.

"Tell me more," she would say. Or, "Am I understanding this right?"

Her questions led me to a deeper level of understanding of whatever was bothering me. It was healing to be listened to with such attention. Somehow, her simple act of surrounding the problem with loving awareness transformed it—transformed *me*.

Part II

Do You Know Jesus?

9

"Five dollars for the haircut. Fifty dollars to start your car." That's what my FBI friend, Joe Koletar, said when I told him I was from Youngstown, Ohio. From the 1930s through the early 1960s, Mafia rivals waged car-bombing wars for dominance in Youngstown's bookmaking, race wire service, and numbers game.[1] Most everyone in town bet on the numbers or the horses.

I'd been away from Youngstown for thirty years when Joe made that comment. I'd forgotten the Mafia violence. But I hadn't forgotten the violence in my family home. I was born in 1937, to a family of hard-drinking Irish Catholic steelworkers. My father was a foreman in the shipping department at the Youngstown Sheet and Tube, which was at that time the largest employer in the Mahoning Valley; my uncles also worked at one of the three major steel mills. My mother worked at a department store, and later managed a small furniture store.

Both of my parents had previous marriages. My father had a son, John, who died in infancy, ten years before I was born. My sister Rosemary, eleven years my senior, had a different father whom I'd never met. My father was an alcoholic who either drank to excess or not at all. When he drank, he could become violent.

My first memory. I am two and a half, standing in a crib, watching my older cousins restrain my screaming father, pinning him to the bed nearby.

I am five. My father, mother, and I are in the car. He is driving, and hollering at my mother. I am sitting between them. I feel his arm on my chin as he reaches across me, pushes the door open, and tries to shove my mother out of the moving car.

I am seven. It is Rosemary's high school graduation night. The girls are wearing long white robes, with corsages and white mortar boards. The boys are in black. After the ceremony, Rosemary, my mother, my father, and I are walking down Federal Street, the main street in town. My father is yelling. He reaches out, rips the corsage from Rosemary's dress, and throws it into the gutter.

I am nine. My mother and I are in the kitchen. My father is yelling at her from the dining room. When he appears in the kitchen doorway, she opens a drawer and pulls out the butcher knife. "If you come near me," she says, "I will stab you."

When my father would take me to a ballgame or some other outing, he'd ruin it by stopping at a bar on the way home. A terrible disappointment would wash over me when we pulled up in front of the familiar neon sign, and he repeated his usual lie: "We'll just stop in here for a minute." I'd sit beside him at the bar, my legs dangling off the stool, eating peanuts and pretzels while he drank the first beer and then the second. After a while, I'd protest that I was tired. "Go sit in the booth," my father would say. "We'll be going soon." Then he'd keep drinking while I curled up under our coats and fell asleep.

Every few years, my father and mother would go to the parish priest and my father would "take the pledge"—promising God that he would not drink for two or three years. And he would keep the pledge! During those good years, there would be no violence, no screaming, no marathon sessions at the bar. We'd enjoy being together. He liked me and would kid me. There'd be ice cream and listening to Friday night Madison Square Garden boxing matches on the radio.

We'd go to the Saturday night high school football games with his friend, Dan Moriarty, packing thick wool blankets for the cold and buying paper cones of French fries sprinkled with vinegar and salt. Or we'd drive to Cleveland to watch the Indians or the Browns at Lakefront Stadium, a massive structure that could hold 75,000, but was usually three-quarters empty.

When he was sober, he was kind, even tender. My mother suffered from asthma. On hot summer nights with the bedroom windows open to the pollen, she would wake him, saying, "Sid, Sid, I can't breathe." He would get out the hypodermic and vial of adrenaline, boil the needle in a saucepan, and give her an injection. After a short time, her symptoms would ease. They'd hug and kiss; he'd comfort her.

My father was kinder to Rosemary during the "pledge" years. She dreamed of a career in opera, and studied voice with Mrs. Marjorie Funk Brenner, the president of the Youngstown Music Teachers Association. My father, mother, and I proudly attended Rosemary's solo and group recitals, and theater and opera performances.

Music was Rosemary's lifeline, allowing her to imagine a life beyond what Youngstown could offer. She won local, regional, and state vocal competitions. With her teacher's encouragement, she auditioned at the Metropolitan Opera in New York in 1953, and received a scholarship for advanced training in voice. However, after a short stay at the Metropolitan, she realized that pursuing a career in opera would be incompatible with her other heart's desire—a husband and children.

She later told me that her time at the Met made her understand what the world-renowned soprano Maria Callas meant when she said, ". . . in a woman's life love is more important than artistic triumphs."[2] Rosemary chose love, marriage, and children. She and Bob Laughlin had five children: James, John, Kevin, Kathleen, and Brian.

I gravitated toward sports. In Saint Dominic's grade school, I played in the Youngstown Catholic school football league. I enjoyed being part of a team, and looked forward to playing football for Ursuline High School, like my cousin Edgar. He was all-state. When he graduated, he gave me his football pants. I hung them in our basement, and every few months I'd try them on to see if they fit.

But the summer before high school began, a classmate, Dick Cavanaugh, told me he would be going to high school at Holy Cross Seminary at Notre Dame, in South Bend, Indiana. "South Bend" piqued my interest. My father and uncles were avid Notre Dame football fans. Some of my earliest memories are of watching them load the car with blankets and coolers for the 315-mile drive west. While they shivered in the cold of the stadium, I listened at home on the radio, picturing every play.

If I go to the Holy Cross seminary for high school, I thought, *I might be able to go to Notre Dame football games!*

Although Notre Dame football was the impetus for going to Holy Cross Seminary, I had thought of becoming a priest earlier in grade school. So when I told my mother I wanted to go to the seminary, there was a genuine spark of "vocation" in my desire.

I was fourteen when I entered the seminary, one year after Claire entered the convent two miles away at Saint Mary's. I enjoyed the first two weeks: new friends, walking the Notre Dame campus, being away from the violence at home. Then—homesickness. I had never been away from home for more than a weekend. I called my parents, crying, "I want to come home."

"Oh, honey," said my mother, "of course you can come home."

But after we got off the phone, my parents called Fr. Collins, the seminary superior. He met with me the next morning.

"Son," he said, "why not just stay a couple more weeks and see if you don't feel better?"

I agreed to stay. The homesickness passed.

A month later I attended my first Notre Dame football game. Seminarians didn't need tickets; we showed our IDs, walked right in, and stood behind the last row of seats, under the scoreboard. I was so glad to be there, I didn't notice how stiff my back and legs got from standing through the whole game.

At Holy Cross, the priests who taught us, the religious brothers who maintained the grounds and the buildings, and the religious sisters who cooked and did the laundry were dedicated to our intellectual, moral, social, and spiritual welfare. I thrived in this environment of academic rigor, spiritual seeking, and deep friendship with classmates, an environment so different from the heavy-drinking steelworker culture I'd left behind. This was the beginning of a thirteen-year journey toward ordination as a priest; four years of high school, one year in the Novitiate, four years of college, and four years of graduate school theology.

After graduation, I went to Sacred Heart Novitiate in Jordan, Minnesota for a year of silence, reflection, prayer, and manual labor. In August 1956, I made temporary vows of poverty, chastity, and obedience and became a member of the Congregation of Holy Cross. In September, I enrolled at Notre Dame. My major was philosophy, as groundwork for the requisite four-year graduate work in theology.

One day not long into my freshman year, I was walking back to the seminary after class when two men approached to ask directions to the library. The more talkative one told me that they were going to the library to study commentaries on the epistles Saint Paul wrote when he was in prison. They planned to go to Africa to preach the word. Every few moments, the man asked his companion, "Isn't that right, Cecil?"

After fifteen minutes or so of telling me about his and Cecil's plans, the man looked earnestly at me and asked, "Do you know Jesus?"

I was speechless. Nobody had ever asked me that. I was nineteen, and had been raised Catholic, with weekly confession, Mass on Sunday, Lenten observances, and everything that being Catholic implied. I was training to be a priest and had just pronounced my first vows. I was dressed in a black cassock and elbow-length cape and wore a black-braided cincture cord around my waist and a biretta on my head.

And yet—did I know Jesus? The truth is, I didn't even know what it meant to "know Jesus." I *wanted* to know him. I had prayed over the years, and tried to live by his teaching: *Love one another as I have loved you.* I read what in those days were popular accounts of Jesus' life.

But for all that, I didn't know Jesus in the way he was asking.

As if reading my mind, he said, "You go home. And you read John's Gospel. And you will know Jesus."

After that encounter, I began in earnest to read John's Gospel, the rest of the New Testament, and the Old Testament. I craved the experience of *knowing*, in all its intimacy and directness, that the man I'd spoken with seemed to possess. Yes, I was getting to know Jesus through my academic studies and by trying to make my moral conduct a mirror of his own—but I wanted to know him with my heart.

10

During my undergraduate years, I volunteered with an elderly Holy Cross priest, Fr. Forestall, who had a ministry to the Mexican migrant farmworkers in Indiana's massive corn and soybean fields. Fr. Forestall was an advocate for better wages and working conditions, proper housing, and adequate food and clothing. My classmates and I played with the farmworkers' children, taught catechism, and drove family members to evening or Sunday church services.

I recall a bitter cold winter night visiting with a family in one of the ramshackle migrant cottages. Looking down, I could see the ground through the gaps in the floorboards. I was stunned to see the conditions in which these families lived.

Volunteer work was a bright spot in a junior and senior year of severe depression and anxiety. At first, I merely felt tired—then exhausted. I felt "down." It intensified into unrelenting depression. I did my best to hide my condition from others. Every moment was torment. I never considered suicide, yet I longed for my life to be over. The pain was psychological, spiritual, physical—it followed me from bedroom to lecture hall to cafeteria, never easing.

I lived one day at a time, hoping the depression and anxiety would go away. My academic abilities seemed unaffected. My grade point average was excellent during my senior year, and I was excused from attending second semester classes.

Without classes to distract me or pull me into contact with others, I spent hours at the library, writing a lengthy final thesis on Kierkegaard. He and other existentialists placed a priority on individual existence, on authenticity, and on accepting responsibility for who you are and who you will become. At night, I lay awake, ruminating on the questions raised by his writings.

I understand now that my depression and anxiety were perhaps caused by doubts as to whether I was taking the right direction in life. In August I would be expected to take "final" vows. But should I? Was I on the right path?

At the time, psychological counseling was not readily available at Notre Dame. I confided in my spiritual director, Fr. Henry Fiedler.

"Don't leave," he advised me. "Be patient and take things day by day."

I also spoke to the seminary superior, Fr. Paul Rankin. I had to work up courage to tell him what I was going through. He met me with a blank stare. "I don't understand what you are telling me," he said. I was instantly flooded with shame. Was my condition really so unusual, so freakish, as to merit such an uncomprehending response?

I learned later that Fr. Rankin suffered from chronic depression. My revelation hit a nerve. Perhaps he had not found a way to deal with his depression, so how could he counsel me? He was the "superior," and I was a seminarian. There could be no open dialogue about such a raw and taboo subject.

At the beginning of that year, senior students were required to submit a list of our preferred places to study theology after graduation. There were four options: Washington, D.C.; Le Mans, France (where Holy Cross was founded in 1837); Santiago, Chile; and Rome, Italy. Although there were no "bad" placements, I had wanted to serve the poor in Latin America, and had taken electives in Spanish. I requested Santiago. I was assigned to study in Rome.

Depression followed me to Rome. But the new and stimulating environment eased it slightly. Living in Rome was a heady experience. I enjoyed interacting with the Italian people, walking streets of ancient history, studying the archeology, architecture, and art; visiting the tombs of Saint Peter and Saint Paul; having daily briefings on the issues being debated in the Vatican II Council (freedom of conscience, universal call to holiness, the nature of the Church); studying under the Jesuits at the Gregorian University; being in several small group gatherings with Pope John XXIII, and hearing him speak—at the height of the Cold War—on the need to establish "universal peace in truth, justice, love, and freedom."

Our residence, the Collegio di Santa Croce, was a wing of the international headquarters (The Generalate) of the Congregation of Holy Cross, on Via Aurelia Antica, in the south section of Rome. After years of interacting with mostly white, English-speaking colleagues at Notre Dame, I was now living in our Holy Cross Collegio with priests and seminarians from Bangladesh, India, Canada (French and English-speaking), France, East and West Germany, Latin America, Haiti, Ireland, and the U.S. At meals, we spoke French and, on alternate years, Italian. Lectures at the Gregorian were in Latin.

The Gregorian University was in the heart of the city, between Piazza Venezia (Victor Emmanuel Monument) and Trevi Fountain. Classmates and the Jesuit faculty were from all parts of the world. Living, worshipping, and studying with this international community helped me understand the meaning of the term "Church Universal." I was proud to be part of a worldwide Christian community, and invigorated by friendships with men whose backgrounds were different from my own.

I threw myself into my theological studies, and was especially drawn to personalist theology that emphasized the importance of personal "presence" and "dialogue" between individuals, and between the individual and God. At Notre Dame, I had read Martin Buber, Gabriel Marcel, and other mid-twentieth-century philosophers who emphasized the importance of "presence." In Buber's terms, this meant an ability to say "Thou" to others instead of relating to them as objects, and for Marcel it meant a state of "extravagant availability" in which one puts oneself at the radical disposal of others and of God.

Of all the courses I took at the Gregorian, Fr. Juan Alfaro's course on the Act of Faith was the most meaningful. It helped me understand faith as a personal relationship with God.

In his opening lecture, Fr. Alfaro said, "There are three fundamental mysteries of Christian revelation: The Trinity, the Incarnation of the Word, and the call to participate in the life of God" through the act of faith, which "is an action of the whole person...."[1]

"(It is) the free response of the human person to a personal God who is calling and inviting him to the intimacy of friendship, to a supernatural communication with God, to a mutually free, personal giving . . . . This personal aspect is essential to the act of faith and must never be forgotten. Through the act of faith, the human person makes his first and fundamental 'option' with respect to God, . . . ordering, in a new way, his whole life toward God."[2]

Thomas Aquinas likewise emphasizes the importance of dialogue and encounter in relationships. While Catholic theology teaches, correctly, that faith is an intellectual assent and a personal assent, Aquinas holds that the personal is the most important. He argues: "Everyone who believes assents to someone's words; . . . it is the person to whose words the assent is given who is of principal importance . . . ; the individual truths through which one assents to that person are secondary."[3]

I resolved to cultivate a quality of "presence" when speaking with someone, as a way of serving others in my priesthood. I would offer my complete self to the people I served, in the hope of creating the kind of sacred relationship Aquinas and Juan Alfaro described. Little did I know at that time that when it came to cultivating this quality of presence, my greatest teacher would ultimately be Claire.

II

At our Collegio, I was impressed by how readily the French and French-Canadian seminarians expressed their feelings, and how comfortable they seemed to be discussing personal matters—both things I struggled with.

Following a lecture, they'd get together to share views, and carry on a lengthy and passionate debate: What was the deeper meaning of what the speaker said? How did what he said affect our lives? What were the implications for the Church and for society?

They also formed Bible study groups. I admired how attentively they listened to the readings of Bible passages, their rapt faces expressing a deep-seated belief that they were truly hearing the word of God. In my mind, I believed this too—but not in my heart. After all these years, my faith remained stubbornly intellectual.

Yet thanks to my contact with these friends, I began to listen to the Bible passages with the belief that what I heard did, indeed, have the power to transform me. For the first time in my life, I opened myself to the possibility that if I listened with my heart, Jesus would, in fact, heal me, as he had healed the daughter of the

Canaanite woman who believed in him with all her heart, saying, *Woman, you have great faith! Let it be done for you as you wish.*[1]

I began to read John's Gospel with my heart, especially passages such as when he washes his disciples' feet: *If I then, your Lord and teacher, have washed your feet, you also ought to wash one another's feet. For I have given you an example, that you also should do as I have done to you.*[2]

It was 1962. Pope John XXIII formally opened the Vatican II Council on October 11. Over the next ten months, I had three "personal encounters" that transformed my person and my life: an encounter with a psychiatrist, with God, and with a fellow seminarian.

Dr. Frank Ayd had been invited to Rome as consultant to the Bishops at the Council. He was on the faculty at Johns Hopkins University School of Medicine, and was chief of psychiatry at Franklin Square Hospital in Baltimore. He had just published *Recognizing the Depressed Patient*,[3] a groundbreaking book for general practitioners. He played a key role in establishing the American College of Neuropsychopharmacology, an international organization of leading brain scientists.[4]

He was residing at the Generalate as the guest of the Holy Cross superior general, Fr. Christopher O'Toole.

In an after-dinner lecture, Dr. Ayd spoke to us of his research on medications for mental illness. His father suffered from manic depression, and shortly after World War II Dr. Ayd worked in a Veterans Administration hospital caring for mentally ill veterans. He pioneered the use of chlorpromazine (Thorazine) for patients with schizophrenia and manic depression—an effective alternative to the electroshock therapy his father had once endured.[5]

DO YOU KNOW JESUS?

I attended to his every word as he described the signs and symptoms of depression. *He understands*, I thought. *This man understands me.* It was the first time I heard someone describe what I had been suffering. Relief washed over me. I was not "different." Unlike my seminary superior at Notre Dame, Dr. Ayd would "understand what I was talking about." I had to speak with him.

If I followed official channels and asked the seminary superior for permission to request an appointment with Dr. Ayd, the superior would have to ask the superior general, who would have denied my request.

The Generalate and Collegio were one L-shaped building with a glass partition and unlocked door separating the two wings. After the lecture and Q&A, when everyone had gone to his room, I entered the Generalate, found Dr. Ayd's room number on the marquee, quietly climbed to the second floor, and knocked on his door. He opened immediately. He was in his stocking feet, and without jacket and tie.

"Dr. Ayd," I said, "may I speak to you about something?"

I don't remember how long we spoke. I do remember that he was welcoming. That he listened. And that he affirmed that I had been clinically depressed. He didn't advise me to seek therapy. Instead, he observed that I had come through the most severe phase of the depression, and that the symptoms I was now experiencing seemed to indicate a lifting and easing of the condition.

Being understood, heard, and affirmed by him was a healing experience. I now knew that what I was experiencing was normal and not uncommon. When I left his room, I felt more at peace than I had in years.

A month or two later, I had a second life-transforming encounter. I was in my room one night, reading a book by a French priest, Monsignor Guy. The book was in French, which forced me to read more slowly and with greater attention. The passage was on the meaning of the vow of obedience, and discussed the ways in which Jesus was obedient to God his Father. The example Monsignor Guy chose was Jesus' prayer in the Garden of Gethsemane, the night he was betrayed:

> *He fell to the ground and prayed*
> *that, if it were possible, the hour would pass from Him.*
> *And he said, "Abba, Father, all things are possible for You.*
> *Take this cup from Me.*
> *Yet not what I will, but what You will."* [6]

As I read the words, I felt I was one with Jesus in the garden. I became deeply calm. I realized that God had revealed Himself to me as my Father. I was in Jesus, in the Garden, before "our" Father. I was God's son. I had encountered God as Abba.[7] I knew that all was well, and would always be well, no matter what happened in my life.

Do you know Jesus? This was the beginning of the answer to the question asked of me four years earlier. As my life has gone on, I have tried to know him more. I understand that when we try to love as Jesus loved, he will reveal himself:

> *Those who have my commandments and*
> *keep them are those who love me;*
> *and those who love me will be loved by my Father,*
> *and I will love them and reveal myself to them.*[8]

In the summer of 1963, I had a third encounter that marked the final and permanent lifting of my depression. It was not an instantaneous encounter such as I just described, nor a brief interaction such as I had with Dr. Ayd. It was a two-week companionship with a new friend whose views on the meaning of priesthood were identical to mine.

Holy Cross seminarians studying in Rome spent summers in Fiera di Primiero, a small village of five hundred inhabitants in northeast Italy, in the heart of the Dolomite Alps. It was an idyllic setting, with mountain peaks of up to ten thousand feet on three sides of our residence. We passed our days reading, studying, and writing sermons, which we delivered to our own group for critique. We hiked the mountains—short hikes of a day, or longer hikes of several days.

For two weeks that summer, Holy Cross seminarians studying in Le Mans, France joined our group. Among them was Bob Morin, with whom I bonded instantly. Bob had a quiet smile and easy manner. He was from Montreal, and, though his first language was French, he was perfectly bilingual. We decided to spend a few days in the mountains, hiking the trails that wound through pastures and across glaciers.

During the strenuous climbs, we talked about prayer, the priesthood, and what it meant to be Christian. Bob had been a Little Brother of Jesus, men under vows who live in city neighborhoods, hold ordinary jobs, and spend hours of prayer in adoration of the Eucharist. He was also drawn to the worker-priest movement—a radical missionary initiative in which priests worked in factories and other blue-collar occupations, in order to be close to the people they served.

Bob and I shared the understanding that a priest is the

servant of all those he will meet. We discussed Cardinal Suhard, former archbishop of Paris, who argued that the vows of poverty, chastity, and obedience should "make the priest wholly accessible" to those he serves, and we discussed Saint Paul's message to the members of the church at Philippi: *Do nothing from selfish ambition or conceit, but in humility count others more significant than yourselves.*9

To hear Bob talk about how for him being a priest meant serving the poor, learning to pray as Jesus prayed, and making the Eucharist the center of his life, fueled my idealism. It was thanks to these conversations, conducted as we huffed along streambanks and picked our way up rocky slopes, that I felt the last of my depression fading away. Life seemed vibrant and full of hope. Whereas I'd spent years mired in self-doubt, I now felt optimistic about my ability to serve others as a priest, and inspired by the path that was revealing itself to me.

12

On March 14, 1964, I was ordained to the priesthood at our Collegio, along with classmates Bob Ware and Leonard Paul. My mother flew to Rome for the occasion thanks to a gift, I later learned, from a classmate's family. Louise Cavanaugh came with her. It was Louise's son, Dick Cavanaugh, who had started me on this thirteen-year journey when he'd made a casual remark that he planned to attend the high school seminary at Notre Dame.

In July, I sat for my final oral examinations. I was sad to leave Rome, and the international group of seminarians who had spurred me to experience so much growth.

It was routine for newly ordained priests of the Indiana Province to spend a "pastoral year" at Notre Dame before receiving their initial, and usually long-term assignment. After celebrating my first Mass at my hometown church, Saint Dominic's in Youngstown, I returned to Notre Dame.

The usual pastoral year was a blend of light study, saying Mass on Sundays in nearby South Bend parishes, and working with students on social justice initiatives. In addition I was chaplain of Morrissey Hall, a residence for 230 male undergraduate students for whom I celebrated Mass, heard confessions, and offered counseling. It was a privilege to be at Notre Dame as a colleague of fellow Holy Cross priests, faculty, and staff.

That year, my father came for a football game. The rector, Fr. Tom McDonough, gave him a room in Morrissey, and told him he could park behind the hall—the royal treatment, as far as my father was concerned. I'm not sure what made him prouder—the fact that I was now an ordained priest, or that my being at Notre Dame gave him parking privileges that he could only have dreamed of in the 1940s when he and my uncles made the annual pilgrimage from Youngstown!

Despite the fact that I was surrounded by students and colleagues, loneliness began to set in. During my years in seminary, I'd always lived in community. Seminarians did everything together: prayer, volunteer work, sports, vacation, studies, meals. We were a family.

Now I was, or felt, alone. Fr. McDonough was welcoming and encouraging. Fellow priests welcomed me as part of the university community. But this was a different kind of "community." Each person lived in his own assigned residence on campus. When we came together for meals, they were quick affairs, after which everyone went in his own direction. On holidays, many priests went home to their families—while I had come to believe that Holy Cross *was* our family!

I felt this change most acutely on Christmas Eve, my first winter back from Rome. After volunteering to hear confession at Midnight Mass, I wandered over to Corby Hall, the residence of Holy Cross priests who teach at the university. I thought that other priests who had not gone to their families might gather there to celebrate the night. However, the common room was empty. I went downstairs to the self-serve snack bar. No one there.

I served myself some ice cream. University President Fr. Ted Hesburgh walked in. We wished each other a merry Christmas. But it was apparent he didn't intend to stay. After an awkward attempt at conversation, he left, leaving me to finish my ice cream alone.

As I put my bowl and spoon into the dish tub, I thought, *This is not the way I want to live.* I missed the friends I'd made in Europe, and wondered if they were also experiencing a shock of loneliness in their transitions from seminarian to priest.

To counteract the loneliness, I volunteered with the Council for the International Lay Apostolate (CILA), a Notre Dame student group that organized and carried out summer projects to help needy people in the U.S. and Latin America. I agreed to be chaplain for the summer 1965 project scheduled to work in Tacámbaro de Codallos, Michoacán, Mexico. Drew Kershen, a senior from Hereford, Texas, was the very able project leader.

During the fall and spring semesters, Drew and our group met once a week to practice our Spanish, share what we had learned from our readings on Mexican history and culture, and discuss what we wanted to achieve in Tacámbaro.

We agreed to build a house for a family in need, and rebuild a failed septic system. We would also assist a doctor, work at an avocado cooperative, volunteer two afternoons a week at a boys' orphanage, and teach English at the local seminary. We were ten: Drew, Jim Birmingham, Hal Boersma, Jim Murray, Dave Robbie, Mike Rosing, Fred Schnur, Bob Walsh, Mike Witte, and me.

South Bend to Tacámbaro is a 2,170-mile drive. We drove a tan VW van and a Ford station wagon loaded with personal belongings, work clothes, and some of the construction equipment: shovels, trowels, and bags of cement mix. It was an enjoyable drive. A lot of laughs, a lot of singing along with whatever came onto the radio—the Beatles, Louis Armstrong, Janis Joplin, the Byrds.

Tacámbaro is located on the side of a mountain, about 5,400 feet above sea level. Avocados and other tropical fruits grow on the lower slope where the town is situated, with apples growing in the cooler upper regions. We arrived at about six in the evening, tired and sweaty after two long, hot days on the road. Fr. Luis Morales, director of social services for the diocese of Tacámbaro, welcomed us and introduced us to the two women who would cook for us and do laundry. He then took each of the students to meet the families with whom they would live.

The next morning, after breakfast and Mass, we headed to Colonia, the poorer section of town, to begin work on the new house. The house's foundation was stone and cement, the walls cinderblock. It had a log roof. When completed, the house had electricity and running water, including a shower and toilet. Although none of us were expert builders, we had the advice of some local carpenters.

One afternoon, I had to pick up more cinderblocks. A Colonia resident agreed to come with me. We got in the van, and I asked him if everything was clear for me to back up. In a nearly inaudible voice, he said, "Hombre!" I wasn't sure what he meant. Was he starting to say something to me, and then stopped? Or was he saying "hombre" the way we might say "man" at the beginning of a sentence, like "Man, is it hot!"

I asked him again if it was all clear to back up. Again he muttered, without any emotion, "Hombre!" I got out of the van to see if I could safely back up. A man was lying under the passenger side rear tire, his eyes closed and his breath smelling strongly of booze. Had I shrugged off my helper's remark and backed up, I would have rolled over the man and killed him.

While this tragedy was avoided, another occurred that has remained in my heart—and likely in the young men's hearts all their lives. One of our group, Mike Rosing, a Holy Cross seminarian, drowned.

On the Fourth of July weekend, some of the students decided to go to Playa Azul, where the Rio Balsas flows into the Pacific Ocean. Although I considered going with them, I wanted to visit the Parícutin volcano and the remains of the church of the village of San Juan Parangaricutiro, so they dropped me off in Uruapan on their way to the coast.

When they arrived at Playa Azul in the evening, they noticed a restaurant on a sandbar a short distance offshore. It was low tide, and they saw they could easily walk there. But in the morning, the tide was high, and Mike and Fred decided to swim. As soon as they got chest deep, they were caught in a powerful riptide created by the strong outflow from the Rio Balsas. Although Fred made it back to shore, his breath ragged and his body limp with exhaustion, Mike disappeared under the water.

Drew and the other two students ran to a group on the beach who had a small motorboat. The group was from a French construction company building a dam on the Rio Balsas. They immediately launched their boat and found Mike's body trapped in branches adjoining the sandbar. They drove the group, with Mike's body, to the police station in Ciudad Lázaro Cárdenas.

The police questioned everyone about the circumstances of Mike's death. The police chief prepared a death certificate stating basic facts of the drowning. Drew signed the death certificate: July 4, 1965. The French company flew Drew to Uruapan, along with Mike's body.

When I returned to the hotel that evening, I found on my dresser a note from Drew asking that I call him immediately. Amid sobs, he told me that Mike had drowned.

We called Fr. Hesburgh. He gave us the name of a Mexico City funeral director, and said that someone from Notre Dame would call to tell him that I would bring the body for embalming to return to the U.S.

Drew called Mike's parents. He expressed his and our group's condolences, and told them how Mike's body would be returned.

A funeral director in Uruapan placed the body in a makeshift coffin, and a driver and I set off for Mexico City, a nine-hour drive.

I was in shock. The trip seemed endless. The driver spoke only his native Indian language; my Spanish could not bridge the gap between us. Donkeys and other animals would wander onto the road, causing the driver to brake quickly, and the coffin would crash into the back of my seat. Each time the coffin hit, I thought of Mike's parents. What could I say—what could anyone say—to comfort them?

In the middle of the night, the driver turned into a small town, pulled up behind a completely dark building, exited the truck, and went into the building. I was frightened. I didn't know where I was, who I was with, why he had left the truck. After about half an hour he came out with two other men who told me we had to switch trucks. They moved the coffin to another truck, and we drove away.

As we neared Mexico City a large interstate-type sign hung over the highway: "MEXICO." And the driver exclaimed "MEXICO!" as though we were approaching a sacred shrine. I was matching map coordinates (pre-GPS) to find the street to the funeral home. When we approached the street, I signaled the driver to turn. As he did, I saw the sign, "Sentido Único (One Way)," and flashing lights behind us. Police.

The officer came to the driver, who indicated he didn't speak Spanish. He pointed to me. The officer came to my door, nodded at the street sign, and was silent. I explained our situation. That a young American had tragically drowned. That we had driven all night and were now only fifty yards from the funeral home.

The officer told me to exit the truck. When I did, he just stared at me. Then he said that my problem was of no concern to him. His concern was that we had committed a traffic violation, and that it would cost us before he would let us go. I paid his bribe, and we found our way to the funeral home.

I spent the night in a nearby hotel. The next morning I returned to the funeral home. Mike's body had been embalmed and placed in a dignified casket. The funeral director opened the casket so that I might see the body. He said, "Doesn't he look beautiful?" I couldn't comprehend the question. *Beautiful?* I thought, *This young man has died. His parents, two thousand miles away, are grieving his loss. There is no beauty here.* I nodded and thanked him.

Our group remained in Tacámbaro; we continued to build the house and carry out our other commitments. We talked constantly about Mike. Although there were moments when each of us wanted to be home, finishing our mission gave us time to grieve together; to process his death in a way that would not have been possible alone. When our Tacámbaro work ended, I returned to campus. The others went home until the start of the new semester.

Visiting Mike's parents was one of the most difficult things I have ever done. I had thought of them constantly, from the moment I learned he had died. We sat in their living room. I wanted to comfort them. We cried. I don't remember what I said, or what questions they asked. They didn't ask, *Why were you not with the group?* They didn't say, *If you had been there, our son would be alive.* But the unasked question, the unspoken statement hung in the air. I felt an overwhelming sense of guilt. I found no words of comfort; no words to ease their grief.

When they returned to South Bend, Drew and the others visited Mike's parents. Drew told me the Rosings were kind and accepting in their grief. But the fact that Mike was gone left a void in the living room that no words or tears could fill.

Years later, I told Drew that I still felt guilty for not being with the group that day. He comforted me by saying there was nothing I or they or anyone could have done to save Mike. "Fred was an athlete, in excellent condition," he told me. "And even he was barely able to swim to shore against the riptide."

Mike's grave is in the Holy Cross community cemetery at Notre Dame, in the first row inside the gate, and facing the Dome. I visit his grave when I go to Notre Dame. I have his memorial card and, though Drew's words were comforting, I still carry lingering guilt that, had I been with the group, I might have advised against trying to swim to the restaurant. And they may have agreed. Or I might, foolishly, have gone into the water with them![1]

13

Shortly after my return from Tacámbaro, I learned that the Provincial Council had recommended that I continue studies for a Ph.D. The objective was to become qualified to teach at Notre Dame. Like Claire, I felt a surge of elation at this news—followed swiftly by reservations.

At that point in my life, I had been a student since I was six, except for my novitiate year in Minnesota and pastoral year at Notre Dame. I was ready for a change.

"Fr. McCarragher," I said, "I appreciate the offer. But first, I'd like to work for a while."

I explained that this would allow me to give back to the community that had educated me, and give me time to think about what I wanted to study for my doctorate.

He agreed. Two months later, he told me I would be chaplain of Saint Edward's University, a small liberal arts school run by the brothers of The Congregation of Holy Cross in Austin, Texas—just across the Colorado River from where Claire was teaching at Saint Mary's Academy.

After completing my remaining responsibilities at Notre Dame, I boarded a Greyhound bus for the eighteen-hour ride to Austin. I was happy to be working instead of studying. I enjoyed the mild winters, though summer temperatures sapped your strength. It was 98 degrees at ten o'clock the night I arrived.

My first responsibility was to celebrate the opening Mass of the 1965 University school year. Saint Edward's did not have a choir, so I asked Fr. Jim McDonough, my Dominican colleague, what to do for music.

"Why don't you call the sisters at Saint Mary's Academy?" he suggested.

The sister who answered my call said, "Saint Mary's Academy, this is Sr. Helen Bernard speaking." "Sr. Helen Bernard," I said, "I'm Fr. Jim Callahan, the new chaplain at Saint Edward's. Fr. McDonough suggested I call to ask if your high school girls could sing at the opening Mass of the Saint Ed's school year." "Oh, Fr. Callahan, you need to speak with Sr. Ellenice," she said. "Hold on, I'll get her."

That was my first conversation with Claire (Sr. Helen Bernard); nothing remarkable. Nothing that would lead one to think we would marry five years later.

The day of the Mass was bright and sunny. Students poured through the doors of the dining hall, where the Mass was held in lieu of the chapel, to accommodate the large number of attendees. I wore my priest-black suit with the Roman collar. Later, Claire would tell me we met on the dining hall steps, before the Mass. She said, "You looked so clean." I didn't remember the moment.

I do remember the reception, after Mass, at a student residence hall. Claire was seated on a couch, talking and laughing with some of the Academy girls.

"Sr. Helen Bernard," I said. "Thank you so much for bringing the choir. They sounded wonderful."

She turned back slightly to look up at me. Her face was luminous. Joyful. I noticed her aliveness. At the time, my noticing was faint—I didn't make much of it. It was only later that this appreciation would turn into love.

AS CHAPLAIN, I was responsible for religious services, and engaging students in social justice and other volunteer projects in the Austin community—such as participating in Cesar Chavez's march to support migrant farmworkers, and visiting patients at the Austin State Hospital alcohol treatment ward. I also said daily and Sunday Masses in the university chapel and student residence halls, heard confessions, and made myself available for discussions with students in the dining hall and other campus venues. Even though I wasn't much older than the undergraduates I mentored, I knew they looked up to me, and I did my best to be worthy of their trust.

Fr. Joseph Rick was my superior. Born and raised in Texas, Joe was six-foot-five, bald, and about 230 pounds. He walked with a limp from a hip injury incurred during his forty years as a missionary in Bangladesh. A maverick, he had gotten his pilot's license before entering the seminary, and on his ordination day in Washington, D.C., when he learned, to his delight, that he would serve in East Bengal (later, Bangladesh), he rented a plane and buzzed the seminary.

So I was only mildly apprehensive the morning I went to his office to tell him I'd gotten a speeding ticket the previous night while driving home from San Antonio. He gave me a knowing grin and said, "Son, you have to keep checking ahead for radar, and in the rearview mirror for cruisers."

I had a bedroom in the Brothers' faculty residence, and an office and adjoining bedroom and bath in a freshman residence, André Hall. When someone in the university president's office reprimanded me for having given a homeless man my André Hall room for the night, Joe said, "Next time, rent a motel room for the person you want to house, and we'll pay for it." He was a good man. He gave me every support I could have wanted in my work and personal life.

Absorbed in my tasks as chaplain, I didn't think of Claire again until we both started to volunteer at the Travis State School for mentally handicapped men, a large complex situated on 430 sandy, mesquite-covered acres in the farm country east of Austin. From the first moment I set foot there, I knew it was a special place. Although I'm sure the institution had its share of problems, there was an atmosphere of love and joy that I've rarely encountered in similar settings.

There were 1,800 men, many of them nonverbal. They were clean and well cared for. When you introduced yourself to one of them, he would lower his head, so you could fold back his shirt collar and read his name. They won my heart with their innocence and sense of fun.

Claire and I visited the School on Sunday afternoons, along with our respective contingents of Saint Ed's and Saint Mary's students. We made the visits as interactive as possible, engaging the men in songs, games, and storytelling—anything that would give them a moment in the spotlight.

On one occasion, Stevie raised his hand to ask if he could sing a song to the group.

"Absolutely, Stevie," I said. "Come up beside me and sing." He eagerly walked to the front of the room, and with a big smile and even bigger voice sang, "Happy birthday to me, happy birthday to me, happy birthday, dear Stevie, happy birthday to me."

We applauded and sang it back to him, his smile getting bigger and bigger.

On a rainy, chilly Palm Sunday, I asked if anyone knew the story of what happened to Jesus during Holy Week. Eddie, standing against the cinderblock back wall, nodded. I asked, "Eddie, would you like to tell us the Holy Week story?" He shook his head, a definite "no."

I said, "Would you like to stand beside me, while I tell the story?" A nod "yes."

He joined me. I began the story, starting at the Last Supper. I described the room where they had the meal, and how Jesus and the disciples were seated at the table, how Jesus washed their feet and told them to love one another.

I asked Eddie, "And then what happened?" He said, "Then they went to a garden." "What was the name of the garden?"

"Gethsemane."

"And what did Jesus do in the garden?"

"He prayed to God."

"And what did the disciples do?"

"They fell asleep."

"And then what happened?"

Eddie told the rest of the story—not just the passion and trial and crucifixion, but also the resurrection and the appearances to Mary Magdalene and the other disciples. Then he turned to me and said, "I've had that in my heart all these years"—as though he had been waiting "all these years" for someone to ask him to tell the story.

DO YOU KNOW JESUS?

At Christmas, we celebrated Mass while seated around a small table in the meeting hall. When it came time for the priest to make the offertory, we gave the men a chance to show or talk about the Christmas gifts they had received. When everyone had had a chance to show off his gifts, we resumed the Mass.

Wham! A heavy leg in a Texas boot came down on the altar. It was Buddy. He had forgotten to show us his new boots. We paused the Mass to marvel over Buddy's boots. Buddy was pleased!

The time I spent volunteering at the Travis State School is a cherished memory of giving and receiving love. While I was so often tormented by striving and questioning, the men at the state school lived in the present moment, fully engaged with the people around them and the moment-to-moment flow of their lives.

It was over the course of those Sunday afternoons that Claire and I became friends, recognizing in each other not only a shared commitment to serving others but a delight in each other's company. Our happiness was apparent to others. When Claire's student volunteer who drove her to Travis State School remarked, "Sr. Helen, I think you're in love with Fr. Callahan," Claire blushed and looked away, and said, "Oh, you must never say that!"

Part III

Transformed by Love

14

During the period we were volunteering at Travis State School, Claire and I met once a week to talk through her hopes, fears, and doubts about leaving the convent. After several months, she wrote to Mother Loretto Conway, the provincial superior:

When we spoke during your Provincial visit two years ago, I shared with you that I was struggling with the question of whether to leave Holy Cross. I have decided to leave in June, at the close of the school year. I respect the Community's right to its way of life, and I too must respect my right to live my Christian life according to my conscience, in a new way. I thank the community for the excellent education and spiritual life it has given me, and I will continue to cherish my Holy Cross friends.

A few weeks later, she met with Mother Loretto in Washington, D.C. to complete the process of dispensation from her vows. On the morning of the meeting, she dressed in her religious habit for the last time, after seventeen years in Holy Cross. As the heavy black habit slid over her head, she felt a shiver of anticipation mixed with sorrow. Today she, Sr. Helen Bernard, would again be Claire Lyons.

Following their meeting, Claire changed into a simple one-piece dress. Mother Loretto gave her a check for $500. How strange it must have felt to walk down the street in plain clothes, with $500 in her purse and few other possessions! That night, she called her parents to tell them of her decision.

Her father made no bones about his opinion. "I hope you have insurance. It's expensive to bury someone, you know." Nellie was quiet, and Claire couldn't tell what she was thinking. Was she proud of her daughter for knowing her own mind? Or was she worried about how Claire would fare in the "real world"?

She returned to Austin to friends who had invited her to stay with them until she found work. She looked forward to a new career path, and the freedom to date, marry, and have children. For the first time since she was twenty-three, she would apply for jobs, buy her own clothes and groceries, and find her own way in the world. It was thrilling—and daunting.

In the 1960s, a woman who left the convent could be stigmatized as someone who turned her back on God. I was concerned about how Claire would weather the judgments and the severed relationships that were certain to occur. But she had the support of many friends and others in the Austin community—even as some friends broke contact.

On our first visit to Travis State School, one of the "special needs" men, seeing she was no longer wearing her religious habit, remarked, "You retired from being a sister!" Claire smiled and said, "Yes, I have!" I wished for Claire's sake that more people could see things the way he did. A woman's decision to leave the convent was an evolution of her faith, not a betrayal or abandonment.

Although Claire had little in the way of financial or material resources, she had her college degree, years of teaching experience, and a drive to succeed. Most importantly, she had her faith. I admired the calm and competent way she set about getting her life in order: borrowing money from the credit union to buy a car, poring over job postings, and enrolling for a master's degree in counseling psychology at UT, financed by a $700 student loan with a $16.00 a month pay-back fee! I had enrolled in the same program the previous year.

A few weeks after UT classes began, Claire became ill with pneumonia. She needed hospital care, but didn't have health insurance.

A Lebanese American couple, Dr. Herbert Nassour and his wife, Hoda, had a twelve-bed charity hospital adjacent to Saint Ed's. A friend told Dr. Nassour about Claire, and he admitted her. When I visited, she was pale and wan, and anxious about whether she would be well enough to attend classes, let alone find a job. I brought her the papers to request formal withdrawal "for medical reasons." She would receive an "incomplete," rather than a failing grade, and could be reinstated when she returned to class.

Then came an unexpected breakthrough. Sandy Nassour, Dr. and Mrs. Nassour's granddaughter, had been Claire's student at Saint Mary's Academy. Sandy's mother visited Claire in the hospital, and when she learned she had been looking for a job, she offered to get her an appointment with the director of the Texas Office of Personnel Management.

They met with the director a week after Claire left the hospital. He began the conversation with, "I really don't have jobs to offer you, Ms. Lyons." Claire's heart sank, and she thought, *This is going to be nothing more than a courtesy visit.* Then he said, "But I can tell you of openings in the Texas civil service system for which you qualify. One might interest you. The Travis County Adult Probation Department has a probation officer opening."

Claire's ears perked up. She thought of her students in Hell's Kitchen, many of whom had likely ended up in the prison system. She applied for the job, and a few weeks later she received notice to appear for an interview at the Travis County Courthouse.

When she arrived, she saw several candidates seated on the long, wooden benches outside the interview room. Claire was the only woman. Once again, her heart fell. This was Texas in the 1960s. What were the odds they would hire a woman to work with convicted felons, let alone a woman with no experience in criminal justice? Still, when it was her turn to face the interview panel, she was confident she would do well. Perhaps she would have been less confident had she known that there were no female probation officers in Texas at that time. If hired, she would be the first.

After introducing himself and the panel members, Giles Garmon, director of the Probation Department, said, "We recognize that you do not have experience in our field, and we are interested to know why you applied for the position."

In her teaching years, Claire had encouraged her students to think through and form opinions on important issues. In preparing for the interview, she had rehearsed answers to the questions the panel would likely ask, including the question of what her views were on probation. She was well prepared.

Later, Giles told Claire that she had described his own understanding of the barriers people face following a criminal conviction, and of the ways a well-run probation program can benefit the community, not just the offender. Rather than seeing her sex as an impediment, he was eager to hire a woman who would add a new dimension to the department's development. I remember the excitement in Claire's voice when she called to tell me she had gotten the job.

She was responsible for supervising probationers who had committed crimes that are today classified as third-degree felonies: deadly conduct with a firearm, DWI (third offense); state jail felonies (burglary, criminally negligent homicide, prostitution). Probationer supervision included weekly or monthly individual meetings, monthly group sessions, meetings with probationers' families, and coordination of probationers' alcohol or other drug rehabilitation with state and federal treatment programs. In less than a year, she was promoted to supervisor and given responsibility for training and supervising new officers.

This was Texas in the 1960s, just years after the passage of the Civil Rights Act. There was deep racial prejudice against African Americans and Mexican Americans. Giles hired the first African American probation officer, Gerald Henderson. Claire was his supervisor. On a drive to visit a probationer at home, Claire and Gerald stopped for gas at a "Full Service" station.

Claire waited for the attendant, but he never came. She got out of the car and waved to him inside the station, but he ignored her. Gerald said, "It's because of me." A white woman with a Black man didn't go down well in Texas.

Claire was named director of volunteer training. I became a volunteer, and Claire and I co-led the probationer group therapy session one evening a month. After our meetings, we would walk along the Colorado River, or stroll on the statehouse grounds. I never grew tired of hearing stories about her probationers, which were always colorful and often moving.

Tommy was on probation for breaking into cars to steal radios and car phones. One morning, Claire was late for Tommy's appointment. "Tommy," she said, "please excuse my being late. I had locked my keys in the car." Without missing a beat, and not seeing the irony, Tommy said, "Oh, Ms. Lyons, you should have called me. I would have gotten you in like *that*." And he snapped his fingers.

One of Claire's most touching stories was about Tanisha.

It was the end of a long night. Tanisha and two fellow prostitutes were walking home. A man drove up and waved a twenty and a single dollar bill out the window. The women agreed to say yes, and then roll him. However, the man knew their names. After they robbed him, he reported them to the police.

At Claire's first meeting with Tanisha, she tried to reach her "feeling side" to generate some motivation toward "changing her lifestyle." She asked, "How do you feel about what you did?"

Tanisha put her hands on her hips, threw her head back, and announced, "How do I feel? Seven dollars! He expected each of us to go with him for seven dollars! I don't go on no date for seven dollars!"

Her professional pride had been offended. That's how she felt!

Tanisha came faithfully for her appointments and would talk at length about her life, her difficult childhood, and her string of dead-end relationships. At a reporting session several months into her probation, she said, "Ms. Lyons, I wants to be like you."

Claire replied, "What do you mean, Tanisha?"

Tanisha said, "Ms. Lyons, I wants respect."

Claire almost cried. She said, "Okay, Tanisha, let's start with the clothes. The Spandex has to go!"

Tanisha came to the next session wearing something less clingy. She lost considerable weight, and began to look healthy and happy. She successfully completed her probation. She found a steady job and married—on her terms. When her fiancé proposed, she said, "Yes, on one condition; that you stop drinking and are sober for at least a year." She told Claire, "I put him on probation!"

15

For the first time since leaving the convent, Claire felt independent. Thanks to her steady income, she could rent her own place—a room and bath with kitchen privileges in a private home on Harris Boulevard, a ten-minute drive to the probation office and UT campus. She did her shopping at Granny's Attic, where she could buy secondhand clothes on "lay-away," and replaced her oil-burning Ford Pinto with a used Oldsmobile Cutlass Supreme.

For a couple of years now, Claire and I had been involved with Nova Cor—an annual dude-ranch weekend retreat for thirty students from local Catholic universities. We would wait for each other after our small group sessions, just for the joy of walking to the plenary sessions together. In the late evenings, we would stroll to the end of the lush, rural property and, with one foot on the split rail, lean on the fence and joke about how we were looking out over the "lower forty."

In those moments, I was filled with longing. I was a priest; I had taken a vow of celibacy. Although I knew that the energy sparking between Claire and me was nothing less than love, I wasn't sure what the existence of that love meant for my life.

For months, I struggled with this dilemma. As a priest, I wasn't supposed to fall in love. Should I tell Claire? Say nothing and hope the feeling went away? Should I break off our friendship, and take myself out of the path of temptation? Did she have similar feelings about me?

Having entered the seminary at fourteen, I had dated only a couple of times, and had never experienced the full-body rush of being in love. Now, I smiled whenever I thought of her. I found myself replaying our conversations in my head, and listening to music that reminded me of her.

When I finally had the courage to tell Claire I loved her, the words came out all wrong. We were walking across the UT campus one afternoon in late November, and I blurted, "Claire, I'm falling in love with you, but I can never leave the priesthood." As soon as the words were out of my mouth, I was kicking myself. Was there anything *less* romantic than what I had said? I thought about Claire night and day, yet here I was, delivering a statement someone might write in a report!

Still, it was good to acknowledge my feelings. We had an awkward conversation, each of us struggling to express how we felt about each other. "I love you too," Claire said carefully, "but I know you'll never leave the priesthood. Of course not."

We agreed that there was no way we had a future. And yet here was this love, impossible to ignore, impossible to pursue.

On a cold, gray, misty December day, we drove to Lake Travis, twenty miles northwest of Saint Ed's, to talk over "our situation." I told Claire I had reached a decision. I couldn't see her anymore.

The expression on her face was calm, sad, unsurprised, without a trace of anger.

"I understand," she said. "The last thing I would ever want would be for you to leave the priesthood."

"So we have no future," I said, my heart aching.

"No," she agreed. "We don't."

A week later, I received a small box in the mail. Inside was a sterling silver medal and chain. The front of the medal was engraved with the Chi Rho symbol, and the Greek Alpha and Omega. The back was engraved with the numbers 12-11-67—the date I'd told Claire I could no longer see her.

Chi and Rho are the first two letters of the word "Christ" in Greek (ΧΡΙΣΤΟΣ, or Χριστός) —Chi (χ), Rho (ρ). Alpha (A or α) and Omega (Ω or ω) are the first and last letters of the Greek alphabet, and a title of Christ and God in the Book of Revelation: *I am the Alpha and the Omega, the First and the Last, the Beginning and the End.*[1] The medal symbolized our shared faith in Christ, to whom we had committed our lives—Claire's way of telling me that she understood my decision.

The next couple of months were torment. Although I buried myself in work and prayer, telling myself I had done the right thing by taking myself out of the path of temptation, the truth is, I was questioning everything. Was the Catholic Church wrong to insist that priests should be celibate? Was there some way to continue my friendship with Claire without compromising everything to which I'd devoted my life?

During the 1968 Easter recess, a faculty member at St. Ed's offered me the use of his ranch for a private weekend retreat. I spent my time there praying and taking long walks in the mesquite. As much as I tried to put Claire out of my mind, I realized how much I enjoyed being with her, and wanted to be with her. When I returned to Austin, I called and asked her to have lunch with me. At that point, we'd been apart, with no communication, for about two months—but now, we unofficially began to date.

We didn't use the word "date," of course—it wasn't part of our vocabulary. We just wanted to spend time together, without worrying too much about what it meant or where it was going. After spending so long wracking our brains for a solution to "our situation," it felt good to forget about solutions and just enjoy each other.

So how do you date when you aren't permitted to date?

Out-of-the-way places. Enjoying the Texas scene: roadhouses with sawdust on the floor and country and western bands or music boxes. Dancing the Texas Two-Step at the Broken Spoke, or the Silver Dollar, or the Dry Creek Café, with the menu scrawled in black crayon on the white refrigerator. Truck stops.

Parties at Jerry and Lynn Milsap's and other probation officers' homes for holidays or birthdays, where we'd dance and sing "Cowtown" and other country and western songs. Horseback riding at Danny's ranch. To be more intimate, at Claire's room on Harris Boulevard.

Or out of town at Lake Travis, swimming, lying on the blanket. On the way out, we'd stop and I'd buy a six-pack and Fritos. In the evenings we'd talk, smoke, and kiss on the sunporch overlooking Austin, when Claire's landlady was away. I'd go home at five in the morning!

Or in Galveston at the Hilton that jutted out into the Gulf.

Or at the Huntsville Prison Rodeo, where female prisoner Candy Barr sang "I got fever" and wiggled and danced atop a farm wagon on the rodeo floor, with the men, in white uniforms, going wild behind a caged-in section of the stands set aside for prisoners.

I recall how, at her apartment, we knelt facing each other, pretending we were children, telling each other of our childhoods. It was as though we wanted to start our lives over; go back to the beginning and together role-play growing up—as though we wanted to heal each other of the hurts of our past. We held our arms around each other and looked happily into each other's eyes.

I was thirty-one. Although I'd felt love for my friends and for Christ, the intensity of this romantic love completely bowled me over. It was like a fever, impossible to resist. I *had* to see Claire, had to be with her, had to hear her voice. The intensity of these feelings allowed me—allowed *us*—to live in a state of total contradiction. I was a celibate priest, and yet I was dating a woman. Claire wanted a husband and children, and yet she was dating a man forbidden to marry.

That summer, my mother intercepted a letter Claire had sent me at my parents' home, in which she wrote of our plans to spend a weekend at her sister's place in Cape Cod. My mother became hysterical, convinced that I would bring shame on the family. Rosemary had to slap her to make her calm down.

A few days later, my father told me that my mother was concerned that I might leave the priesthood, and that she had asked a priest in confession what she should do.

This was the first "adult" conversation I ever had with my father. We were in the garage. He was tinkering on his car while a ballgame played on the radio. For some reason, the news of my relationship with Claire made him open up to me in a way he had never done before. He talked about his first marriage and divorce, and about his son, John P. Callahan, who died at less than a year old. I wasn't quite sure what he meant for me to take from all this. That life was filled with sorrows, regrets, and paths not taken? That love was scarce and should be cherished where it could be found?

I assured him that I did not foresee leaving the priesthood. Yes, I was in a relationship with Claire, but it would not lead to marriage. With a grunt, he closed the hood of the car, and I understood that the conversation was over.

Several months later, in February 1969, my mother was hospitalized with congestive heart failure. I took leave of my UT course and flew to Youngstown. As I stood at her bedside, I realized that we'd never truly known each other as adults, and now we never would. Our relationship had been strained ever since she'd found out about Claire. I consoled myself with the fact that I had *not* left the priesthood—nor was I planning to. The scandal my mother feared had not happened. Her son was still a priest. I said her funeral Mass at Saint Dominic's parish.

That evening, my father and I sat at the kitchen table. "You don't have to worry about my drinking," he said. It was almost an announcement that that was what he intended to do. I returned to Austin. He sold the family house and spent the money on gambling and drink. He remarried and divorced, eventually became sober, and started ushering at Saint Dominic's. He met Marie Borne, a gentle and loving woman, and they pooled their Social Security checks and shared a two-bedroom apartment for many years. I was happy that he had found sobriety and comfort in their companionship.

16

By the spring of 1969, Claire and I had completed the coursework for our master's degrees. I applied for and received a fellowship in marriage and family therapy at the Institute for Religion and Human Development at the Texas Medical Center in Houston, intending to complete a Ph.D. Every weekend, I made the 330-mile round trip to visit Claire in Austin, staying at her apartment.

Although Claire and I tried to fully enjoy our love, discussions about our "situation" inevitably crept into our talks. Claire was forty. She wanted a family. She had dated after leaving Holy Cross, before she and I began to date, and a husband and children were very much in her plans. Though I was in an intimate relationship with her, I still could not make the transition in my mind from intimacy to marrying.

The realization that I *wanted* to marry Claire came suddenly that summer in Austin as I was driving down First Street toward the city. *If I don't make up my mind soon, I'm going to lose her*, I thought. *Another man will come into her life, and I'll spend the rest of my days regretting my foolishness for turning from her love.*

I thought of Dante's words when he realized he was in love with Beatrice:

*I have just set foot on that boundary of life
beyond which no one can go, hoping to return.*[1]

From that moment, there would be no returning from the awareness that my heart's desire was to marry Claire. I could no longer deny it, repress it, or undo it.

But the path from *wanting* to marry Claire to *deciding* to ask Claire to marry me was complex and painful.

I had to reconcile in my conscience that I had taken a vow of celibacy but that I now wanted to break my vow and marry. And I had to grow into a new emotional orientation to a life of marriage, possible family, and service in a secular occupation. I had to reset my emotional mindset developed over eighteen years of seminary training and active priesthood.

Priesthood in the Church was my life's goal. It was my identity. It was how my family knew me; how friends and the community at large knew me. It was my work, my profession. My purpose in life. Why I existed. God's call.

But was I called to celibacy? I had promised to be celibate, but could I be?

Was I reneging on the commitment I had made to be celibate, to give my "whole person" in service to God and others?

THE CATHOLIC CHURCH'S doctrine on conscience is liberal. However, its pastoral attitude toward members who follow their consciences is often severely strict and contrary to its doctrine. The Church teaches that "Man has the right to act in conscience and in freedom so as personally to make moral decisions."[2] "Man has in his heart a law inscribed by God. To obey it is the very dignity of man; according to it he will be judged...."[3]

When I was chaplain at Saint Edward's, Dr. Nassour asked me to meet with a seventy-year-old alcoholic and mentally agonized patient, Charlie Donovan. Dr. Nassour thought that Charlie might find in me a sympathetic ear for the many years of emotional torment he had suffered since he had left the active priesthood forty years earlier. We met several times in my office to talk, listen to Irish music, and enjoy each other's company.

One afternoon, he told me, in sobs and tears, how he was treated when he left the clerical priesthood. Charlie said, "When the chancellor of the diocese handed me my dispensation papers, he said, 'And may God have mercy on your soul!'" Charlie reached out to me. I took him in my arms and began to cry. He sobbed and sobbed. A broken man.

Claire invited Charlie to Thanksgiving dinner, along with other guests who had no local family.

To obtain a dispensation from my vows, I had to submit several documents to the Vatican, including a letter to Pope Paul VI to ask that he "laicize" me (change my status from "cleric" to "layman"), and grant me permission to marry. My letter read:

After four years of intense prayer, reflection, and conversation with my spiritual director, I have come to the clear realization that I cannot any longer live the celibate life.

I wish, therefore, respectfully to request from your Holiness a dispensation from my final vows, laicization with release from all obligations of the priesthood and permission to marry. I request free-

dom to marry with the full blessing of the Church so that I may remain a practicing Catholic.

I have deep love for the Church, her Eucharist, and her Priesthood. In the future, should a married clergy be permitted, I would, with full joy, desire to serve the Church in this capacity.[4]

After signing the letter in the presence of my provincial superior on October 15, 1969, I called Claire and cried. I cried because I had taken the first official step to surrender the priesthood as the Catholic Church defined it: a celibate life of total service to God as an ordained minister of the Church. It took several years to live comfortably with that decision.

I knew I was called to the priesthood. And I knew that, once a man is ordained a priest, "The vocation and mission received on the day of his ordination mark him permanently."[5] I had been ordained. I would always be a priest. But I would not be able to live out "the vocation and mission received on the day of (my) ordination . . . ." My decision about celibacy was clear. I now had to live my priesthood as a married man.

When I signed the letter, I knew it was the right thing to do. It was what I had to do, to live with my conscience in peace and love. As Elaine McGillicuddy wrote of her late husband, Francis, a diocesan priest who married:

> *You wrestled with conscience, and*
> *both of you won:*
> *Deciding to leave the clergy,*
> *you chose integrity.*[6]

Claire and I decided that, rather than move forward immediately with my dispensation request, I would seek a leave of absence from my provincial superior, find a job, and give my decision to leave the clerical priesthood one last test.

We also agreed that, if we married, we wanted to live somewhere other than Austin. In the 1960s, Austin was a smaller and more intimate community than now. We preferred not to be a newly married couple encountering situations where someone would say to Claire, "Didn't you used to be Sr. Helen Bernard?" Or to me, "I think I remember you from my visit to Saint Ed's. You were chaplain there, weren't you?" We wanted a fresh start.

"What about Atlanta?" Claire said. "It's supposed to have a wonderful arts scene."

Neither of us had ever been to Atlanta. But we decided to try it, based solely on what Claire had heard!

I wrote to the chancellor of the Houston Diocese: *I want to ask you to hold the documents in your office until I ask you to send them to Rome. My Provincial has given his permission to support myself for the next six months or longer. I want to use this time to put a final check on my decision.*

A fellow Holy Cross priest, Fr. John Foley, invited me to stay with him at Atlanta University, where he was the Catholic chaplain. Through John, I met several clergy and laypeople who were supportive of my circumstances. One man, who had terminal cancer and whom I visited regularly, bought me a suit for job interviews!

I had no clear idea of the type of work I wanted. My endeavor was to "find a job"—hardly a good career planning strategy. In a pre-internet job-search world, I followed every newspaper job opening ad, and made random visits to Atlanta companies' personnel offices. I also made an appointment with a personnel recruitment firm.

About ten "personnel specialists," seated behind gray metal desks, were interviewing clients. I don't recall the details of my initial interview. But what happened next changed my approach from "job search" to "career definition." My "personnel specialist" told me that the director of the office wanted to interview me.

The director didn't have a job opening. But he asked me a question I had failed to ask myself: "When you boarded the plane in Austin, what type of work did you envision doing?" I hadn't "envisioned" anything. I needed income. I might have taken *any* job. Now, I realized that I wanted a job in which I served people in economic or other type of need.

While driving with John to a meeting, we passed the Atlanta Area Technical School Job Training Center. The next day, I met with the center's director, Jack Shoemaker (retired Army colonel). There was an opening for a job placement counselor, and he offered me the position. Jack was a gracious man. Though I was qualified for the position, I suspect he was Catholic, knew I was taking a new direction in life, and wanted to help me.

Irony. One day, I am looking for a job. The next, I am hired into a position to help young people, mostly inner-city Black males, find work that matched the skills they were learning in the training center: welding, carpentry, plumbing, and other trades.

I don't recall that I was an effective counselor. My office was located near the training floor where heavy machinery was always grinding away. I had difficulty hearing the trainees. And they spoke a dialect of English I had a hard time understanding. I did my best.

On a day off, I accompanied John to his meeting with the chaplain of the Georgia Mental Health Institute, a teaching hospital for Emory University Medical School's Department of Psychiatry. The chaplain mentioned that there was an opening for the director of the NARA (Narcotic Addict Rehabilitation Act) program.

It was a civil commitment program funded by the National Institute of Mental Health, of the U.S. Department of Health and Human Services in Washington, D.C. The addicts in the program had histories of drug-related arrests and imprisonments. With the most recent arrest, they could choose prison time or enroll in the NARA program, under a strictly supervised treatment and rehabilitation regimen. Perhaps the fact that my resume showed I had volunteered with felon offenders (many of them addicts) with Claire in the Travis County Probation Office tilted the interviewers to favor me.

With an adequate income, I could find a place of my own. On Claire's suggestion, I visited the Emory University Student Housing Office, where I saw a listing for a small cottage at the home of Dr. and Mrs. Robert Hatcher. Carolyn Hatcher answered my call. She agreed to hold the listing to give me time to look it over. It was the right size: one room large enough for a chair, sofa, table, and bed; an eat-in kitchen; a toilet and shower; and a screened porch.

I wrote to the Houston Diocesan chancellor: *Please proceed with my request for laicization. I have spent the last few months re-thinking and re-evaluating my decision, and I am fully satisfied that this is the right and correct decision.*

The night I mailed the letter, I called Claire and asked her to marry me. It must have been a vague proposal, because she told her secretary the next morning, "I think I am engaged."

17

When I told Fr. Jim McDonough that Claire and I planned to marry, he said, "If the Catholic Church takes this love thing seriously, we're in trouble." As I write this fifty-three years later, I continue to appreciate the wisdom of Jim's remark. If the hierarchy of the Catholic Church accepts an adult's decision to love according to his or her conscience, the Church will have to accept in full communion divorced and remarried members, gay married couples, priests who choose to marry, and others. I suspect the pews would be fuller, and the congregants more joyful—and that the spirit of love would increase in the Church.

Not long after meeting with Jim, I had lunch with Fr. Walter Dalton,[1] the director of the Catholic Student Center and Newman Foundation at UT. I asked Fr. Dalton if he would allow us to marry in the Student Center chapel. He agreed. A few days later, he wrote to Claire, congratulating her on our engagement: *Happy days! I was most pleased that two fine people have been able to get together. Fondly, Walter Dalton.*

Although we'd had the support and encouragement of many in our community, support was not unanimous. My friend Fr. Bob Morin, who had meant so much to me since we first met in Italy, never spoke or wrote to me again. Claire's best friend during her years in the convent became markedly cool. Our mutual good friend, Fr. Bob Perry, said "No" when we asked if he would preside at our wedding—and he never saw us again, even though he visited Washington, D.C. several times during the thirty years we lived there.

These rejections made us even more grateful for the friends who stood by us.

We married on August 29, 1970. Giles Garmon escorted Claire down the aisle. Fr. McDonough presided. Frs. Lundy and Znotas con-celebrated the wedding Mass. Claire wore a simple white dress and veil. The Student Center choral group provided the music. Our friend from Saint Edwards, Brother Dunstan, read the first scripture passage:

> *My beloved lifts his voice,*
> *he says to me,*
> *"Come then, my love,*
> *my lovely one, come.*
> *For see, winter is past,*
> *the rains are over and gone.*
> *The flowers appear on the earth.*
> *The season of glad songs has come,*
> *Come then, my love,*
> *my lovely one, come.*
> *Show me your face,*
> *let me hear your voice;*
> *for your voice is sweet*
> *and your face is lovely."* [2]

We spent our wedding night at the Houston Shamrock Hilton, and made wonderful, joyful, passionate love.

In the morning, we had a long drive ahead of us, and hadn't slept. When I called room service for breakfast, I asked that they "Send up lots and lots of coffee!" The attendant asked, "How much do you want? We have twelve-cup pots, thirty-two cup pots, and sixty-four cup pots!" Our honeymoon continued to New Orleans, Fort Walton Beach, and on to Atlanta.

Two weeks after we arrived in Atlanta, I ran into Fr. Pat Mulhern, a priest I had met three years earlier at Our Lady of Gethsemane Trappist monastery in Kentucky. We invited him to dinner. Pat introduced us to Ann and Joe Pitra, who became lifelong friends.

Ann and Joe had six children: Julie, Jennifer, Molly, Sarah, Joe, and Katie. I have never been more energized by children than by the Pitra six. They'd be gathered at the door the minute we arrived, all talking at once and asking questions, with smiles that still give me joy to recall.

Ann often invited us to dinner, and on each occasion, we met new friends. The first were Nancy and Paul Koshewa and their children Allen, Kathryn, and Max; soon after, we met Art and Peg Fessenden and their children. The dinner conversations were engaging. Sometimes, the volume rose and rose, especially if Art found something to take exception to. Regardless of the mix of guests, the topic of discussion, or the volume, the evenings were enlivening, enlightening, and refreshing.

Equally enjoyable were the many evenings we spent with them and their eldest daughter Julie watching the political talk shows or sitcoms, especially *All in the Family*, while Ann folded piles of laundry.

Their friendship and the continuing friendship of each of their children and their families has been one of the greatest blessings of our lives. It is not possible to be sufficiently grateful to such loving friends.

Claire and I were happy and in love.

Despite the joy and love we felt, every now and then there came a brutal reminder of the Church's poor "pastoral" attitude toward priests who chose to marry. Eight months after we married, the following article appeared in the *New York Times*.

ROME, April 8—*In an unusually bitter homily during Maundy Thursday rites today, Pope Paul VI likened defecting priests to Judas. The Pontiff, his voice shaking as if in anguish, said that many Roman Catholic priests requested release from their ministry "for vile earthly reasons." He deplored the "moral mediocrity" of those who would renege, like the betrayer of Jesus, on their voluntary promise to serve.*

"I know! I know!" the Pope exclaimed. "One must distinguish case by case, one must understand, be compassionate, forgive, maybe wait for the return. And one must always love."

Pope Paul, recalling the Last Supper and Judas's betrayal, quoted Saint Mark (Chapter 14, verse 21): "It were better for him, if that man had not been born." Dropping the customary pontifical "we," he went on: "I cannot think of that tragic Easter drama without associating it in my mind, as a bishop and pastor, with thoughts of the abandonment, of the flight of so many brethren in the priesthood." Defectors, "whether unhappy ones or deserters," are by their ordination "priests in eternity," regardless of their external social status, he maintained.

The congregation was asked to pray "for those runaway brethren and for the communities they deserted and scandalized," and above all for the ranks of new priests filling the vacancies.[3]

I felt nauseous reading those words—as if the pope had personally condemned me for my "vile, earthly" ways. I remembered the way Charlie Donovan had cried in my office, and the way my mother cried bitterly at the thought that her son might "fail" as a priest. Claire and I had done the right thing. We chose to be faithful to our love, and allow ourselves to be transformed by that love.

Part IV

Helpin' Han'

18

Shortly after we moved to Atlanta, Claire took a position as a psychologist at the Georgia Regional Psychiatric Hospital. It was not a "come-into-my-office-and-tell-me-your-problems" type of job. She worked in a locked unit for suicidal, severely withdrawn, or assaultive patients. She was responsible for collaborating with the patients and staff to develop the patients' treatment plans, supervise the administration and evaluation of their care, and provide individual and group therapy.

As she wrote in her master's degree thesis, "Behavior therapy was the hospital treatment modality. It is based on the premise that behavior is learned. Maladaptive behavior can be modified, and healthy behavior can be learned through giving rewards for acceptable behavior and disincentives for harmful behaviors.[1]

"The rewards were praise, encouragement, affirmation, and 'tokens' (punches on a token card) given when patients behaved in accordance with the agreed treatment plan.[2] Disincentives were notices to the patient that the behavior was not in accord with the agreed plan; or the loss of tokens, through 'negative spending.'"[3]

Emily was one of Claire's most memorable patients.4 Claire said, "I heard Emily before I saw her: 'Gimme my up-on-time tokens, or I'll throw this wastebasket over your head.' When I entered the day room, Emily was standing in front of the nurse's desk with the ever-present token card in one hand and the ever-present plastic purse grasped tightly in the other.

"Emily was nineteen, five-foot-seven, and weighed 175 pounds. When she was nine, her mother burned to death in a home heater explosion. Her father, a violent alcoholic, placed her with her grandmother. When she was thirteen, her grandmother committed her to the central state hospital at Milledgeville. Her diagnosis was 'schizophrenic; chronic, undifferentiated type, and retarded.'"

Claire recalled, "She was obese, and walked as though she were a person with disabilities, bouncing from wall to wall. Threat was her response to efforts to help her change her behavior. She feared men, 'because of what they can do to you.'

"She saw herself as 'Numeral' (her word for neuter). 'I'm not a man or woman, I'm numeral.' She preferred interaction with metal objects, because '(I) never had one hurt me. I'm an elevator mechanic and I am made partly of metal.' Her imaginary husband owned a big steel mill, and they had metal children."

When Claire first introduced herself, "she stared at me and did not respond. She had an oval-shaped face. Her lips were pressed together tightly. She had light brown eyes, about the color of her hair. Her shoulders were broad, and she was wearing a pair of men's pants, a colored jersey, and a pair of old sneakers. Her skin was clear with just a few freckles on her nose. Emily was pretty, though one eye seemed a bit out of focus."

Claire respected Emily's wish to not interact. ". . . (T)here was a fragility, a delicateness about her. I sensed that her hostile behavior was the flip side of her fear and timidity [and] that my approach to her must be gradual. She was almost totally lacking in social skills or feminine behavior. Emily looked on the world and persons with fear and mistrust, her response pattern seemed to be 'strike first and then test, test, test.'"

In her twice-weekly therapy sessions with Claire, Emily initially chose the chair farthest from Claire's desk. In one early session, she came over to Claire and said, "I think I'll call you 'Han.' I asked her why. She lifted my arm from the desk, and though she had no eye contact, replied, 'Because you're just such a Helpin' Han, Mrs. Callahan.'" She began to sit beside Claire at the desk in following sessions.

"Initially, Emily engaged in 'crazy talk'—wandering from subject to subject. Over time, she began to speak of her childhood trauma, her mother and father, her fears, her desires." She learned to physically touch Claire's hand without fear, and even with enjoyment of this modest expression of intimacy. Eventually, Emily took part in group therapy sessions.

Claire and Emily had "girl talk sessions" on "acquiring basic social skills, interest in and knowledge of the appropriate way to dress and put on make-up. Emily learned through behavior rehearsal, modeling and role-playing."

Claire demonstrated and had Emily practice how to appropriately cross her knees, how to keep her legs together when seated. How to wear a dress and walk in high heels. How to wear her hair. How to speak more clearly and softly. They worked on losing weight. And on discontinuing the use of snuff.

"The changes in Emily's grooming and her pride in her

newly discovered femininity seemed to have a spread of effect to almost all of her other behaviors."

Progress was not straight-line. There were setbacks. For example, when Claire arrived the morning she and Emily were to begin work on extinguishing her obsession with metal, Emily was standing at her office door. She said in a loud, hostile voice, "I have something to say to you." Her eye contact was steady.

Claire said, "She asked me if I had a car and did that car give me comfort. I replied that my car was very useful, and I enjoyed it. 'Do you have a husband and a home?' I told her I did. She looked at the watch on my wrist and asked if I liked that watch and did it give me comfort. I said I liked it, it meant a great deal to me, that it had been a gift.

"Emily stared at me and said, 'And you ask me to give up the only things that give me comfort. Well, you can keep your tokens and you can keep anything I could buy with them, 'cause I'm not going to give up the only things that give me comfort.'"

Claire was surprised by the intensity with which Emily rejected the plan, but was encouraged by the fact that Emily was starting to articulate her wants and needs, and relate them to Claire's. In forming her explanation of why she should not give up the metal objects that brought her comfort, Emily put herself in *relationship* with Claire—and that was a huge milestone in her recovery.

"Knowing I was responsible for the plan, she decided to use reference to metal objects in my presence to punish me or to show her anger. She would stand in front of my office and sing, over and over, 'Oh, I've Got a Wonderful Set of Burgle Bars.'[5] Gradually this type of testing and attention-getting diminished as I continued to ignore her when she was inappropriate, and invited her in when she was appropriate."

Over the course of a year, Emily gained more freedom. "She would be rewarded with five tokens each day she went to the hospital cafeteria, or attended the hospital school. Initially, she was accompanied by an aide. She was frightened at first but began to enjoy this new freedom, and even began to go alone.

When she had earned thirty-six tokens, she said she wanted to exchange them for money (seventy-two dollars) to buy clothes.[6] This provided an opportunity to take her off the hospital grounds and experience the larger community.

"When Emily and I met to prepare the shopping list, I suggested that we could purchase a pair of culottes. Her reaction was immediate, 'You can't piss easy in 'em!' I pointed out that 'piss' was a word one did not say in public. Emily responded by saying, 'Don't worry, Mrs. Callahan, I'll be good.'

"She told me she would like to buy a pair of overalls because they had big pockets. I pointed out that overalls were men's clothing, and we were going to buy girls' clothing. Emily agreed.

"Accompanied by a male aide, we drove to the department store. Emily got out of the car, came over and took my hand, and clung to me.

"When we arrived at the lingerie department, I explained to the saleswoman, a woman of about sixty, perfectly coiffured and elegantly dressed, what we needed; that we wanted to begin by buying underclothes and then purchase pajamas, shoes, and a couple of dresses, but that we had a limited budget. The saleslady looked apprehensive when she learned Emily was a patient at Georgia Regional.

"We began by purchasing bras. The saleswoman took us into the fitting room and asked Emily her size. Emily said, '44-D.' The woman replied, 'Honey, I think that is too large for you. Perhaps we should try a 42-D.' That was acceptable to Emily and the saleslady told her to bend over while she snapped the bra.

"Emily obediently bent over, looked up at the saleswoman, and said, 'Can't get the tits in!' A moment of silence followed. I thought, *Perhaps Emily is not the only one who is learning today; maybe the saleswoman has something to learn about social deprivation.* After that I relaxed and told myself I should stop requiring Emily to act like a debutante but acknowledge that she was a young woman who was truly 'coming out' for the first time.

"The shopping trip was a success. Emily got, among other things, a yellow sundress with huge pockets, and the three of us celebrated with a sundae. When she returned to the unit, she insisted on carrying all her treasures herself. She displayed them on her bed, and the staff, and some patients, came to admire them. Emily modeled the clothes and enjoyed every minute of the attention and rewards of her hard work."

It came time for Emily to leave the locked unit. Claire could hear the commotion in the hall, and saw Emily come from the day room, her arms filled with her possessions, her face tense; but her walk determined.

"She stopped at the front door, and we looked at each other. She said, 'Would you unlock the door for me?' I would like to believe that Emily had chosen me specially for that privilege, but she was too single-minded at that point. Emily was eager to begin life on an open unit.

"I unlocked the door and watched her walk, still loping a bit, toward her new, less-restrictive unit. I thought about Emily's last words and knew that many doors had been unlocked for her, that her metal world had been more confining than the single bolt that had just been turned."

In Claire's encounter with Emily, beauty met beauty. Emily's beauty lay deep within; Claire's beauty was that she perceived it and worked carefully to draw it out. Claire saw that, no matter how hard Emily tried to hide it, she possessed within her the desires fundamental to health: to share, to love and be loved, to be wanted and esteemed. Thanks to their work together, Emily left the locked ward.

MY WORK WAS AS INTENSE as Claire's. In the early days, we spent our evenings talking about "my" addicts and "her" patients. These talks could sometimes stretch to bedtime. Even though we felt a need to unburden, the effect was that the workday was never entirely over. We were beginning to feel like colleagues or battle comrades, and this cut into the romance of being newly married. We agreed that, once we got home, we would each debrief for fifteen minutes. Then we'd go out or do something to distract ourselves from the day's routine.

The NIMH notified me that my NARA program would be renewed for two more years. There was no guarantee of long-term funding, even though the addiction problem was worsening in Atlanta and nationally. I began to search for a more permanent position, making inquiries at the Atlanta federal regional offices of the Department of Justice, the Department of Health and Human Services, and the Department of Labor. None of these agencies were hiring.

In June 1971 President Nixon created the White House Special Action Office for Drug Abuse Prevention "to concentrate the resources of the nation against the problem of drug abuse." A year later, enabling legislation for the president's order was under discussion in Congress. The legislation would also require that the NIMH's Division of Narcotic Addiction and Drug Abuse become the National Institute on Drug Abuse (NIDA).

When I spoke about this with the NIMH staff person who oversaw my NARA program, he told me this meant that the federal government would add to its drug addiction research and treatment programs a new initiative to train doctors, nurses, and other health care professionals to recognize and treat substance use disorders, and create a new workforce of drug counselors and paraprofessional ex-addict counselors. The NIMH had set up a prevention and training branch and was hiring staff. "Why don't you send your resume to Dr. Richard Phillipson?" he suggested. He's the head of the new office in Washington."

Before marrying, Claire and I talked about where we wanted to live. "Well," she said, "I can tell you where I don't want to live: New York City and Washington, D.C." She wasn't a fan of big, crowded cities; laid-back Atlanta was more her style. Now, with the feasibility of a job offer in Washington, we faced the first important decision of our married life.

Should we move to D.C. for a job that represented a once-in-a-lifetime opportunity for me to be effective on a national scale, even if it meant living in a place that Claire already knew she didn't like? Or stay in Atlanta, where we'd made friends and where Claire had made inquiries about getting her Ph.D. at Georgia State University?

We agreed that I should take the job, if offered; that we would go to D.C. for five years, and that, if we found we were not happy, we would pursue other options.

When I met Dick Phillipson, I knew I wanted to work for him. A short, energetic man twenty years my senior, he was born and educated in Dublin, and served in the medical corps during the World War II Africa campaign. He was a member of the British military mission to Russia for discussions with Stalin and the Soviet leadership. He retired as brigadier general and chief of psychiatry, and was decorated with the Order of the British Empire for valor in the assault on Monte Cassino. I knew that, under him, I could grow professionally and personally.

At the end of the day-long series of interviews with Dick, the division director, the institute director, and others, Dick offered me the job. That evening, I called Claire. "Love," I said, "will you go on this journey with me, even if it means moving to D.C.?" Without hesitation, she said, "Yes, I will go. I will gladly make this 'our' journey."

19

Claire and I drove the 542 miles from Georgia to Washington in tandem, meeting up at gas stations and rest stops. Two weeks later, we were living in a tri-level rental house in Silver Spring, Maryland. I started my new job on May 31, 1972, while Claire continued to work on her master's degree thesis.

I soon learned that the startup of a new government organization meant planning and executing on the run, working shorthanded, and pushing to meet deadlines on priorities that were constantly shifting. In my first weeks at NIMH, our Prevention and Training Branch (a staff of three!) sent out notices to all U.S. medical schools and other health professions schools, community clinics, and addiction treatment programs, announcing that the federal government would accept applications for grants to train researchers, physicians, nurses, counselors, ex-addict counselors, and others.

But just as we were getting that project underway, word came from the White House that $50,000 substance use prevention grants were to be awarded immediately to Boy Scout troops in states key to President Nixon's November presidential re-election. Boy Scouts don't vote, but their parents do! Our team of three had to set aside the personnel training announcements and turn our attention to soliciting grant applications from Boy Scout troops. The applications would not be reviewed for evidence of quality and success, as is the standard procedure when applying for a federal grant. They would be awarded simply on application.

This and other hairpin turns would have created chaos had the branch chief been someone other than Dick Phillipson. He was team-oriented and had no hidden agendas. Whenever he gained information, positive or negative, in his meetings with senior management, he shared it with my colleague Margaret Wilmore and me. He'd come back from a management meeting and say, "Come in and shut the door." And he'd lay it all out—including his humorous take on the issues.

While the workload was demanding and the atmosphere chaotic during the election months, I looked forward to going to work, knowing that, once the Boy Scout detour was behind us, we would be engaged in something important for the country, and that my day with Dick and Margaret would be enjoyable.

Meanwhile, Claire was making progress on her thesis, and surprised both herself and me by falling in love with Washington. She had lived in Alexandria, Virginia and Washington when a Sister of the Holy Cross. But living in Washington as a married couple allowed us to enjoy the community in a richer way.

Our first friends were Dick and Barbara Phillipson. As a retired British officer, Dick had reciprocal membership in U.S. officers' clubs, including the Club at the Bethesda Naval Hospital. Once a month, when the Docs of Dixieland played, Dick and Barbara invited friends to a dinner and dance.

We looked forward to these evenings. Claire especially enjoyed being with Polly Kaim, a pianist and painter who was loving and unpretentious. Sam, her husband, was chief of addiction psychiatry at the U.S. Department of Veterans Affairs, and later led a research team at the National Academy of Sciences. We also met and became lifelong friends with Jim and Janet Vennetti, a former diocesan priest and nun who had married and had two sons, and with Margaret Wilmore.

We found a vibrant community at Holy Trinity parish in Georgetown. The liturgies were joyful celebrations, and the sermons were intellectually and spiritually challenging. After the Sunday morning Mass, there were religious instruction classes for the children. For adults, there were lectures as well as meetings of committees working on social justice issues such as housing for the homeless.

We attended a prayer group at John and Annie Hisle's home in Bethesda, and I found a sense of belonging in the Holy Trinity Men's Group. The group met from 7 to 8:30 a.m. on the first and third Saturday of the month. After fifteen or twenty minutes of general socializing over bagels and juice, we would move to a living room or family room and gather in a circle. There was no leader and no assigned discussion topic. After a few minutes of quiet, someone would speak.

He might talk about a personal or family problem, a job-related issue, an article he had read, or an incident that had occurred. In the twenty-five years that I participated in the group, we spoke openly with each other, listened, discussed, disagreed, cried, and laughed (a lot). We became friends and remain friends. The group continues, post-Covid, on Zoom.

Meanwhile, Claire found community among current and

former Sisters of the Holy Cross, many of whom lived in the Washington metropolitan area, and with work colleagues.

We felt affirmed in our decision to move to Washington. We enjoyed the political intrigue of Watergate, the constant conservative-liberal struggles, changes of administration, and the inaugural parades. We began to spend time at the Smithsonian museums and art galleries—not just to see the exhibits, but to take courses in history, dance, archeology, painting, and other subjects taught by people from government, private industry, and nearby universities. We attended summer concerts on the steps of the U.S. Capitol, and concerts, ballets, and operas at the Kennedy Center. Strolling hand-in-hand down the crowded streets, we felt we were the luckiest people alive.

In the late summer of 1972, Claire learned she was pregnant. She was overjoyed. At forty-four, she knew that time was running out for her to have a baby, a dream she'd had to set aside during her years in the convent. She told me that if the child was a boy, she wanted to name him John, after her brother. Although I felt anxious about becoming a father, my excitement grew in response to Claire's.

But in November, she had a miscarriage.

It was the first time that deep sorrow touched our marriage. Although as a priest, I had counseled Saint Ed's faculty couples who had experienced miscarriages, it was a different thing to process that grief with my own wife. The morning after the miscarriage, we did something we had never done. Hoping to find comfort, we opened the Bible at random. The passage to which we opened was:

TRANSFORMED BY LOVE

I came from the Father and have come into the world; again, I am leaving the world and going to the Father.[1]

Claire and I understood this to refer to our unborn baby. We took solace in the idea that our child was communicating with us, somehow; letting us know that all was well. Claire was heartbroken, and in the days and weeks that followed I did my best to support her; still, I felt powerless to ease her pain.

We regretted not having children—initially, she, more than I. But as the years passed, we spoke often of the sadness of our loss. I understood more and cried for the depth of Claire's suffering. On one occasion, Claire said, "Jim, we didn't have our own children, but in our work, we have helped many. They will be our children in heaven." As I write this, I know that Claire is surrounded by the loving presence of the people whose lives she touched—and has been reunited with the child we lost on that November day.

20

Claire received her master's degree in December, and, in the spring semester, accepted the position of school psychologist at Good Counsel High School, an all-boys school in Wheaton, Maryland. Returning to work helped ease the sorrow of the miscarriage. And it wasn't long before she was telling me stories about her sessions with parents, and with the boys.

One senior came to ask her, "Mrs. Callahan, can you help me with my nerves?" He was experiencing depression and anxiety triggered by a massive case of acne on his chest and back, which made it hard for him to date or fit in socially. The pain kept him from sleeping, and he was ashamed to let anyone see it, especially girls. Claire gave the boy my dermatologist's name and phone number. He successfully treated the acne. At senior prom, the student brought his date to meet Claire. She was stunningly beautiful, and the boy beamed with pride.

Good Counsel faculty also shared their personal and family worries with Claire. One teacher said she was concerned about her five-year-old daughter, who had become withdrawn and was having trouble sleeping. Claire said she would be happy to talk with her.

The girl was nervous when she came to see Claire, and would barely speak. Claire asked her if she liked stories. "Yes," she said. "Would you like us to play 'Let's make up a story?'" Claire asked. The girl agreed. "Okay," Claire said, "I'd like to play that too. Why don't I start? I'll say something, and when I finish, I'll say 'period,' so you'll know it's your turn. And when you finish, you say 'period,' so I'll know it's my turn." Claire continued, "Okay, here I go. There once was a pretty little girl who could not fall asleep at night. Period." Girl: "The little girl wanted to fall asleep, but couldn't. Period." Claire: "The little girl's mommy was worried that her little girl could not fall asleep. Period."

This exchange went on until the girl revealed that she could not fall asleep because she was worried her daddy would die when she was sleeping. Following more back and forth, the girl told Claire that she had overheard her mother say to her father, "At the rate you're drinking, you could drop dead tonight."

The father was an alcoholic who had since entered treatment for his alcoholism. Claire helped the girl understand that her daddy had stopped doing what her mommy was worried about—he had stopped drinking. And now she could go to sleep and not worry.

Claire once told me she wished she had become a child psychologist. She had a gift of understanding and relating to children and teenagers. We experienced this in our own family.

My niece Karen Laughlin came to visit with my nephew Brian and their two young girls. Their daughter Jenna was four and a half, and had a significant speech delay. She attended a full-time speech/language preschool program, but was still shy and withdrawn, and rarely spoke—and when she did speak, it was difficult to understand her. Most people either looked to Karen for clarification on what Jenna had said or just ignored her.

On the second evening of their visit, Karen, the girls, and Claire were relaxing in the family room. Jenna and two-year-old Morgan were playing on the floor. Jenna went up to Claire, stood between her legs, showed her the toy she was playing with, and said something unintelligible. Rather than look to Karen for clarification, Claire cradled Jenna's face in her hands, leaned in close so they were eye-to-eye, and asked her to repeat more slowly what she had said.

What happened next was magical. Claire continued to lovingly hold Jenna's face, reducing the world to just the two of them, as they talked back and forth for a couple of minutes. Never had anyone made Jenna feel so important and understood. After those few precious minutes, Jenna changed. She became chattier and more animated. The photo Karen took shows the pure joy on Jenna's face, as the one person who had taken the time to make her feel special cuddles her in her lap.

On the long drive home to Florida, she talked up a storm in the back seat. Karen and Brian couldn't believe the change in their quiet, withdrawn daughter.

AT THIS POINT IN OUR MARRIAGE, something felt off in my relationship with Claire. I felt overwhelmed by the intensity of her emotions. At times, they even embarrassed me. I felt she was always looking to me to confirm or validate her emotional responses, or even take action based on them, and I didn't always want to. When she got emotional—or what felt to me like hyper-emotional—I would shut down and distance myself. This made her feel like she had done something wrong, when she hadn't.

I also was having difficulty adjusting to married life. It was not a question of whether I loved Claire—I did! It was a question of buying and owning, accumulating possessions, and living in suburbia. In preparing for the celibate priesthood, I had never envisioned owning anything, and, during my five years as a celibate priest, I didn't own anything. I belonged to a religious community in which we owned everything in common. I had a car, but only when I needed it—it wasn't mine to keep, care for, and maintain. Nor did I have any possessions other than a few clothes and books. I didn't need to own much, because I lived in residences where the household items were part of the arrangement.

Also, in my years of study for the priesthood and ministry, I had envisioned that I would work in urban, rather than suburban settings. I had told my superiors that I wanted to study theology in Santiago, Chile, and spend my priesthood there, working with the poor. In Atlanta, I worked directly with drug addicts and their families, employers, probation and parole officers, and hospital personnel. Even though Claire and I lived in suburbia, my work was "inner-city," in the emergency room, jail, court, and the boarding houses and streets where the addicts lived.

Now, I was working in an eighteen-story government office building in the middle of nowhere. Helping addicts? Yes. But remotely; by visiting community organizations, hospitals, and medical and nursing schools where doctors and other health professionals were trained with money granted to them by NIDA. I had become a middleman—no longer hands-on.

And now, Claire and I were establishing our own home: buying furniture, draperies, curtains, rugs, lamps, dishwasher, washer and dryer, lawn mower, shovels, rakes, and hedge trimmers.

The reader may say, "Yes? So?"

For me, this type of nesting behavior was a massive shift away from what I'd always wanted my life to be—serving the poor, unburdened by the need to weed a lawn or shop for curtains.

I must have caused Claire considerable frustration and bewilderment. She must have thought, "Who is this man who says he loves me, but really doesn't think we need all these things? How does he think we're supposed to live?"

These differences in expectations led us to argue, sometimes loudly. When the arguments came to an impasse, I'd shut down and back away, while Claire would keep digging, intent on finding a solution. I was burdened by what felt like her relentless probing. For her part, Claire was frustrated by my emotional unavailability.

We started seeing Dr. Angelo D'Agostino,[1] a Jesuit priest psychiatrist at Georgetown Medical School. He asked that, between our weekly sessions, we spend an hour a day at home, talking. But the talking was to be structured. Claire was to talk, without interruption, for thirty minutes. I was to listen. Then I was to talk, uninterrupted, while Claire listened. If we wished, we could then spend time discussing one or more issues she or I had talked about.

For me, this exercise was liberating. It allowed me to explain, aloud and uninterrupted, the reasons for my discomfort with the everyday practicalities of setting up a home, and why

I had trouble dealing with Claire's spontaneous emotional responses.

After our therapy sessions ended, I found I could more easily restrain my impulse to squash Claire's spontaneity. And buying, owning and having a comfortable and beautiful home was never again a problem. In fact, it was a joy to work with Claire to decorate our home where we entertained friends and guests and enjoyed being together. I embraced the bureaucratic yet effective way of bringing help to addicted persons and their families. And I enrolled in the University of Southern California's Doctor of Public Administration degree program, attending classes on weekends at their Washington, D.C. campus.

21

Around this time, I had a falling-out with my sister Rosemary. In 1977, she asked if I would be guardian of her five children, should she and her husband pass away. I was ambivalent, and I said, "Let's talk about it when you and Bob come to visit." They came, but never raised the question, and I didn't bring it up.

A year later, I received a copy of Rosemary's will in which I was named guardian, but Claire was not named. Claire felt hurt and offended by the omission. "How could they name you guardian without even discussing it with me?" she said.

I didn't want to refuse my sister, who had been good to me at every point in my life, paying my high school seminary tuition and supporting my decision to leave the celibate priesthood. But I was wary of taking on Claire and trying to bring her around to a decision where we could say yes. In an act of cowardice, I wrote Rosemary a letter declining her request.

I have always regretted my decision. I know I could have and should have pushed through my discomfort in dealing with Claire's strong emotional response. If I had allowed time to pass, and continued to dialogue with Claire, she and I would have agreed to be guardians. I could then have asked Rosemary to amend the will to include Claire's name. But at the time, my tendency was still to avoid conflict with Claire. In doing that, I hurt my sister.

CLAIRE'S SUCCESS at Good Counsel high school paradoxically led to her resignation. She chaired the faculty advisory board responsible for recommending school policies to the headmaster. The board recommended and Claire supported several policies that put Claire in conflict with the headmaster, especially the board's recommendations on drug use prevention, intervention, and discipline.

The headmaster denied that drug use was a problem. He said, "We don't have a problem here." Claire and the other faculty knew that alcohol and other illicit drugs were widely used. He refused to accept the board's recommendations.

He also denied the faculty request that an emotionally needy junior student be permitted to return for his senior year. She and other faculty had made progress in helping the student gain confidence and modify some of his inappropriate behaviors. The headmaster did not feel the school was responsible for intense remediation. The incident triggered Claire's memory that her brother Phil had been dismissed at the midterm of his senior year at Saint John's Prep in Danvers, because Bernie failed to pay the tuition after drinking away the money.

She could not square the decision against her brother and the current headmaster's decisions with what she believed a

Christian attitude should be. She tendered her resignation. The headmaster accepted it.

A few days after her resignation, Dick Phillipson came to my office to say he had just received a call from the Irish National Council on Alcoholism (INCA). INCA had received a grant from the Ministry of Health to train health professionals to design and manage community-based substance use prevention and treatment programs. The ministry's program would also develop criteria for educating and licensing health professionals to work in alcohol services in Ireland's five regional health boards. INCA asked Dick to recommend someone to offer the first six-week phase of the program.

I said, "Claire would be perfect for that."

"That's what I was thinking," he replied.

Claire was over the moon when I told her. There would be no interview. INCA hired her on the strength of her credentials and Dick's recommendation. Claire and I had traveled to Ireland in 1976 to visit the village and house in which Nana Mahoney was born. She was energized by the prospect of a return trip. For the next five months, she updated herself on the literature and prepared the syllabus.

The sixteen participants were directors or senior staff of regional or local alcohol service programs: nurses, psychiatric social workers, psychologists, counselors, and administrators. Claire had planned the skill development part of the course as interactive and experiential; to engage the participants in team design and presentations, with feedback and role-playing. They would read the didactic content on their own, and discuss it in the group sessions.

When she walked into the training room on the first day,

she saw that the participants had anticipated a more traditional, didactic learning experience. They were sitting at desks, notebooks open, ready to take down every word of the visiting expert. The men were seated on one side of the room, and the women on the other!

"Good morning," Claire said, "I'm Claire Callahan. I'm looking forward to getting to know each of you. Perhaps we can begin by moving the desks to the side of the room, so that we can form a circle of chairs and talk to one another more easily." And with that, Claire started them on a journey that none had anticipated, but that all, in their evaluations, said were the best six weeks of the program.

On the macro level, they engaged in exercises to design a community-based alcoholism prevention and treatment program. On the micro level, they explored the importance of emotions—as individuals, in the counselor-client relationship, in individual or group counseling situations, and as administrators. The Irish culture of the 1970s, especially the male culture, was not comfortable talking about "feelings." When Claire asked one participant, "Liam, do you tell your children you love them?" he said, "No need. No, no need. By my deeds they know I love them."

Others expressed similar beliefs that one need not be expressive about one's personal emotions. Claire didn't belabor the point. She suspected that this was a feeling strongly held by most everyone in the room.

As the days and weeks passed, and the members of the group came to know and work effectively with each other, they also became more comfortable giving one another compliments and sharing their feelings.

HELPIN' HAN'

At a farewell dinner and dance at Dublin's Gresham Hotel the evening before her departure, Claire told the group of the joy it gave her to work with them, to know them—to love them. She turned to Liam, and said, "I love you, Liam." The whole group said, "Say it, Liam. Say it!" And Liam said, "I love you too, Claire."

Claire was radiant when I met her at Washington National Airport. Had they given her take-off clearance, she could have flown home, arms outstretched. Dressed in a fashionable Irish tweed suit, and with a smile that filled my soul, she kissed me and said, "It was a smashing success. What wonderful men and women." In her luggage were two beautiful dresses and, for me, sweaters (that I still wear), Irish walking hats, and a shillelagh![1] We talked for days. It was the happiest I'd seen her since our wedding day, and her joy lifted my own spirits until I felt that I, too, could have flown.

After Claire's passing in 2016, two of the program participants, Liam Curley and Oliver Reaburn, wrote to console me. Oliver said, "I spoke with Liam Curley last evening and we both agreed that Claire was without doubt the person who had the greatest positive impact on our professional lives, and what a great privilege it was that she became our personal friend."

SHORTLY AFTER HER RETURN from Ireland, Fran Cotter, my friend and colleague at the National Institute on Alcohol Abuse and Alcoholism (NIAAA), invited Claire to interview for director of the NIAAA's Health Professions Education Program. The goal was to help integrate the teaching of alcoholism and other substance disorders into the curricula of medical and nursing schools.

Many doctors were uncomfortable talking with their patients about these conditions. A major reason was that doctors had few treatment options to recommend. Antabuse (disulfiram) was the only known medication that could help some problem drinkers, and it had unpleasant side effects. Alcoholics Anonymous was an effective self-help resource, but many patients did not subscribe to its premises, or were reluctant to meet with a group of strangers.

Claire had seen the devastating effects of alcoholism in her family, first in the form of Bernie's violence, and later in her sister's and brothers' problem drinking. In her work in schools and in the probation office, she'd seen how alcohol and other drugs destroy young lives and tear families apart. She'd spoken with broken-hearted parents desperate to find help for their addicted children, only to find that their doctors knew little about the subject.

Now, as director of the NIAAA program, she would help turn this situation around by educating a new generation of doctors and nurses. Like me, Claire would no longer be working directly with clients or patients—a loss she mourned, as I had. However, she knew that her work would alleviate suffering in thousands of lives.

THANKS TO OUR DUAL INCOMES, we could now afford to travel. In 1980, we went to Italy—my first time returning since I lived in Rome. We visited Fiera di Primiero, where I had spent two summers and where Bob Morin and I had hiked the Dolomite mountains. When we went to bed on our first night, there were only a few cars in the piazza in front of our chalet-style hotel.

During the night, a traveling fair of arts and crafts and clothing stalls had set up in the piazza. As we strolled among the stalls, Claire noticed a handsome leather handbag. The vendor greeted us. Claire reached for the bag. He took it from the peg and handed it to her, complimenting her. "Occhio fino!" ("A fine eye." "Good taste.")

He asked if he might have the bag. He demonstrated how the bag could be worn "modo sportivo" ("casually, in sporting fashion"). He placed the strap over his shoulder and walked jauntily away. Then, he turned toward us and said, "O, modo classico." ("Or in a more formal manner.") He removed the strap, placed the bag under his arm, and walked back toward us slowly, erect and dignified. Claire bought the bag.

In Milan, we visited Saint Ambrose's grave and Leonardo da Vinci's Last Supper mural.

Ambrose (340–397) was a bishop and Saint Augustine's mentor. He is buried in the church erected during his lifetime, and first named Basilica Martyrum (the Church of the Martyrs), because it was built where martyrs of the Roman persecutions were buried. It is now known as the Basilica of Saint Ambrose.

It is a fifteen-minute walk from the Basilica to the former Dominican monastery of Santa Maria delle Grazie, where da Vinci's painting of the Last Supper is on display on the dining room wall. At the time of our visit, I had not made an association between Ambrose and the Last Supper painting. But later, I realized that, while they are separated in time, they narrate two aspects of the same mystery. Ambrose emphasized the

Christian call to serve the poor, whom he considered "not a distinct group of outsiders, but a part of a united people to be stood with in solidarity."[2] Jesus, at the Last Supper, washed his disciples' feet and said, *If I then, your Lord and Teacher, have washed your feet, you also ought to wash one another's feet.*[3]

I understood that I have not fully taken part in the celebration of the Eucharist, and my reception of the sacrament is not complete until, by service, I share with the poor my possessions, my time, and my talents. I am fed, so that I can feed others.

On our last afternoon in Rome, we wanted to pray at Saint Peter's Basilica. As we entered the piazza, I spied a short man in a bishop's cassock (black cassock, red trim). It was Theotonius Gomes, from Bangladesh, with whom I had studied in Rome. I ran to give him a smothering embrace. He was four-foot-five; I was six feet. He was in Rome for a worldwide conference of bishops to discuss "The Family and the Catholic Church."

He visited with us that night at our pensione to ask our views on issues under discussion at the Vatican conference. We were honored that he paid us that respect. Years later, on a trip to the U.S., he celebrated Mass for a small group of friends at our home in Bethesda. At that Mass he said, "Because Bangladesh is a Muslim country, we are not permitted to actively attempt to convert people to Christianity. Our approach is to live in love and service, and so attract people to our Christian faith."

22

Claire and I returned to Washington invigorated. Our lives began to pass in a blur of work, social engagements, Sundays at Holy Trinity, and visits to Smithsonian exhibits, musical evenings at the Kennedy Center, or Wolf Trap National Park.

But we were suddenly reminded that life was fragile. On January 12, 1982, my sister Rosemary died. It was her fifty-sixth birthday.

I was at my office, working on my doctoral dissertation late in the evening, when Claire called. "Jim, you need to come home. Rosemary isn't well."

I went home immediately. Claire hugged me and told me that Rosemary had died of a heart attack that afternoon. My brother-in-law, Bob Laughlin, had called Claire a few minutes before she called me, but she hadn't wanted to tell me over the phone.

Rosemary and I were estranged since the incident with the will, but her son Jim was getting married in June and I'd planned to make amends to Rosemary at the wedding. Now, I would never get to tell her how sorry I was for hurting her, and for allowing our estrangement to stretch into five years. I felt sick with guilt and regret. How would I face her children at the funeral, all of them knowing how badly I'd let their mother down?

Two days later, I drove to Cheshire, Connecticut. Rosemary's son John gave me a box of memorabilia she'd saved for me, including letters and family photos. I spent the night before the funeral alone in my motel room reading each letter, looking at the pictures, and recalling our lives. It was one of the longest and saddest nights of my life. I realized I'd taken Rosemary for granted, assuming she would always be there. I'd forgotten how suddenly death could come.

A few months after the funeral, I received a letter from Rosemary's daughter Kathleen. It was filled with vitriol, recounting how her mother had always supported me, and how I had let her down in her time of need—echoing the words Rosemary had said to me when I'd declined her request to be guardian. My ears rang as I read it, and guilt gnawed at my heart. For more than a year after Rosemary's passing, I spoke of her constantly to Claire, and felt fresh waves of remorse whenever something reminded me of her. I still mourn her passing.

Rosemary's death initiated a phase of our lives in which we began to lose friends and family. We had long ago gotten past the "invincible" stage of our twenties and thirties, but it was still a shock every time we received news that another friend or relative had fallen ill or passed away.

IN 1983, CLAIRE AND I went back to Europe, this time to Spain. While sitting in a bar in Segovia drinking our morning coffee, we saw several well-dressed people walk by. We thought they might be heading to a wedding. Then we saw a larger group of well-dressed people walking in the same direction. We asked the bartender what the occasion might be. He said, "It's Corpus Christi!"

Corpus Christi, the feast that commemorates the true presence of Christ in the Eucharist, was a national holiday. We left the bar and followed the passers-by to the cathedral, arriving in time to see altar servers and girls in white dresses come down the cathedral steps carrying baskets of rose petals that they scattered over the streets ahead of the procession.

The bishop led the procession, dressed in robes covered with a richly embroidered cape. Behind the bishop, six men carried a flotilla on which a large monstrance displayed a consecrated host.[1] Following the flotilla were dozens of priests in thickly embroidered vestments, then town dignitaries in official suits and colored sashes, then the army band playing religious hymns and patriotic marches. People lined the streets or leaned out of windows to cheer and bless themselves as the Eucharist passed. The air was sweet with the aroma of crushed rose petals.

I noticed a woman leaning out of a second-story window. The Spanish flag hung from the windowsill. Under the flag, in the sandstone arch, was the inscription *Corpus Christi*. It was a church. I said to Claire, "That woman is the body of Christ!" And we laughed at the coincidence that at this celebration of the Eucharist we would be reminded that each of us is the body of Christ.

Two years later, we returned to Europe to visit Italy and France, reveling in delights ranging from fresh pizza in Florence to taking part in a gypsy festival in Saintes-Maries-de-la-Mer,

Provence, and spending several days in Arles visiting scenes painted by Van Gogh.

We spent our last week in Paris, at the Hotel Madeleine Plaza, on the Place de la Madeleine near the Paris Opera. On our first day, fresh from the gypsy festival, we felt giddy and delighted by life. We checked into our room early, and made love like never before.

BACK IN THE UNITED STATES, real life was waiting for us. My father became ill from throat cancer and could no longer care for himself. Claire and I considered having him live with us, but with both of us at work all day, that wasn't feasible. The Little Sisters of the Poor had a nursing home, the Jeanne Jugan Residence, near Catholic University in Washington. I visited the facility. Residents were well cared for. It was clean. No "nursing home smell!" The finances would work out.

As I was leaving, a sister was coming in. She introduced herself as the nursing home director. I explained why I was there, and she advised me, "Don't bring your father to Washington." She explained that the move would not be beneficial on many levels. In Youngstown, there were family members to visit him. In Washington, Claire and I would be his only visitors. The weather would be different. The newspapers and television news would be different. The sports teams would be different. She was a wise woman who had dealt with dozens of people in the situation Claire and I were facing.

I visited nursing homes in Youngstown. The best, an "upscale" facility, was on the north side of town, close to the hospital where he would be undergoing cancer treatments. It was a comfortable and well-run place, but when I suggested it to him, he wasn't interested.

"They're not my people, Jim," he said. Dad had been a steelworker, and eventually owned a small dry-cleaning shop, Sparkle Cleaners. The people in the "upscale" nursing home were former bankers, lawyers, senior level managers at the steel mills. What did they know about loading an old car with blankets for a football game, pooling your Social Security checks for groceries, or whiling away your evenings in working-class bars?

Instead, he chose Assumption Village Catholic nursing home, which was less comfortable but where he felt more at home. I spent the night before he was admitted at his apartment—Marie had already gone to live with her niece. I cleaned out his closet as he lay nearby on a twin bed, occasionally asking him about keeping or donating a certain item. He looked at me and said, "I don't know how a person makes out who doesn't have someone like you to help." I was grateful for his gratitude.

My cousins, Bob and Pat Miller, and Bill and Louise Miller, invited me to stay with them on weekends when I went to Youngstown to visit my dad.

Only a few months after he entered Assumption Village, I was at Mass in Rockville, Maryland. While in line for Communion, I felt the slightest movement across the front of my body; an "awareness." When I came home, Claire said, "Your cousin Bob called. Your father passed away a few minutes ago."

At the wake, I exchanged hugs and greetings with my cousins and their families, family friends, and friends of Dad whom I did not know. I had been away from Youngstown for thirty-five years, but many who came were neighbors whom I knew and whose children were my friends growing up. One special person came. My dad's brother, my uncle George Callahan.

George was "special" because he was my favorite uncle on my father's side. A role model. He had a big smile and smoked cigars. He was warm and kind. He and his wife Amy and their son Skip lived in Grosse Pointe, Michigan, a well-to-do Detroit suburb. He had been a successful owner of musical instrument stores in Detroit. He drove a Buick and wore a camel cashmere coat, like Babe Ruth! I didn't see him often growing up, only when he came to town for weddings and funerals. Skip had been stationed in Youngstown when in the Air Force. He taught me to drive.

When Uncle George came to the evening wake, he took Claire's hand and said, "I always wondered what you looked like. And I like what I see." After the family luncheon following the funeral, he said to me, "Jim, you gave your father a good funeral. You have a beautiful wife and a successful career. Keep it going!"

Two years later, I visited my uncle. He was retired and living in Flint, Michigan. I stayed three days. One evening he said, "Jim, when I heard you had left the priesthood and married, I was angry. I disapproved. Eventually, though, I said to myself, 'This is Jim's business, not mine. His life, not mine.' And I'm happy you have a lovely wife and a good life together."

I felt a kind of relief at my father's passing. Over the years, I'd tried to forge a closer relationship with him, but his alcoholism made it difficult. About twice a year, Claire and I had visited Dad and Marie in Youngstown, and they'd visited us in Washington. My father and I had gotten along fine on a superficial level, but we never quite forged an authentic connection.

HELPIN' HAN'

BEFORE MY FATHER'S illness and passing, I had left NIDA, because President Regan had cut my programs from the NIDA budget. I took a position at the National Cancer Institute (NCI) to create a national program to educate physicians on how to do a brief intervention to help patients reduce or quit smoking. The goal was to reduce the incidence of cancer caused by tobacco. However, the program never got off the ground.

Four years later, I left government to become executive vice president of the American Society of Addiction Medicine (ASAM), a national medical specialty society of physicians who have an interest in prevention and treatment of alcohol and other substance use disorders. ASAM's goal was to gain American Board of Medical Specialties (ABMS) recognition of addiction medicine as a board-certified medical specialty. Although most addiction medicine physicians were board certified in another specialty (principally, internal medicine, family medicine, or psychiatry), they wanted additional certification to demonstrate they were knowledgeable and qualified in addiction medicine.

Certification was important not only to the physician. It gave patients and their families confidence that their doctor was competent to treat them, and that insurance companies would pay for doctor visits and hospital or outpatient treatment. With this in mind, certification meant that millions more patients would be able to access the help they needed—a fact that kept me highly motivated to pursue ABMS recognition.

TRANSFORMED BY LOVE

IN JUST A FEW YEARS following my move to ASAM, Polly Kaim, Claire's brother Phil, and our friend and my mentor, Dick Phillipson, passed away

I was not comfortable going to visit Sam Kaim the very evening Polly died. I thought we should wait a day or two. But Claire felt we had to go.

When Sam opened the door, he said, "Two angels!"

Sam, Polly, and their son Eddie were not observant Jews. When we came to the house, Sam and Eddie were scanning the Yellow Pages for a rabbi to conduct the service. "You're just the person, Jim. Will you speak at Polly's funeral service?"

It was a large funeral. Sam was well known for his work at the Department of Veterans Affairs and his collaboration with the White House on policies to prevent and treat addiction. Polly was active in the Washington arts community. Both were strong supporters of the Democratic Party and party candidates.

The coffin was in a viewing room. Family and guests were in adjoining rooms. Claire and I wanted to pay our respects. When we stepped into the viewing room, Claire held me back and motioned that we should not enter. Senator Robert Byrd (West Virginia) was standing alone at Polly's casket, his hat in his hand, his head bowed.

Senator Byrd's modesty touched us. He didn't call attention to himself. Had we not noticed him, he may have left as quietly as he had come. Claire told Sam that the senator was with Polly. We left them to their privacy.

In my remarks at the service, I called attention to Polly's

warmth and love, and to the source of that love, her Jewish faith and heritage as expressed by the prophet Micah:

> *With what shall I come before the Lord,*
> *And bow myself before God on high?*
> *He has shown you, O woman,*
> *what is good.*
> *And what does the Lord require of you*
> *but to do justice*
> *and to love kindness*
> *and to walk humbly*
> *with your God.*[2]

The following year, 1991, Claire's brother Phil died of throat cancer at the VA Hospital in Jamaica Plain, Boston. Claire and her brothers John and Joe were at Phil's bedside during the week before his death.

In a letter to Fr. Keyes, who was to celebrate Phil's funeral Mass, she outlined the tribute to Phil that she asked Fr. Keyes to present as his homily. She wrote,

In considering what the family would like to have you say about our brother, we decided that the theme of family love, in its relationship to the Eucharist, was most important and appropriate.

Like every family there are joys and sorrows we could talk about, but the experience of the last six months has affected us all greatly.

Phil was diagnosed with cancer of the throat last Christmas. In his great need he reached out to his family—and his family responded magnificently with an outpouring of love and support.

In celebrating the Eucharist this morning, we are celebrating the love of a family. Christ gives us the strength to love—joyfully and

*generously. And Christ helps us to receive not only his love, but the love and care of others. It is the mutual sharing of love to and from Phil that we celebrate at this morning's Mass. And we celebrate too Phil's release from pain and entrance into eternal peace.*3

After the burial, Claire said the weather at the graveside mirrored Phil's stormy life. Winds were at fifty-three miles per hour with heavy thunderstorms and rain at greater than half an inch an hour.4

Dick Phillipson passed away on October 30, 1993 in Berryville, Virginia.5 His funeral was a small but dignified gathering at Grace Episcopal Church. The weather was pleasant. His daughter Tina and her husband John Harvey came from England. Professional friends, Barbara's son Rob Irwin and his wife Irene, and Barbara's daughter Sarah Irwin were present.

We had lost a dear friend. Claire and I maintained our relationship with Barbara after she moved to an assisted living facility.

As I approached my sixties, and Claire her seventies, we realized we would continue to have reminders of our own mortality.

23

The first reminder was a call from my family doctor. I'd recently had lab work done. He told me that I had an elevated PSA, and he wanted me to make an appointment for a prostate biopsy.

I called Claire. She immediately began to cry. *Jim, what were you thinking?* I scolded myself. *You should have waited to tell her in person.* I wasn't too worried about prostate cancer. I knew that early stage had a high cure rate. But Claire was distressed. "What if it's not early-stage, Jim?" she said.

The biopsy was positive, but the cancer hadn't spread from within the prostate capsule and was treatable. However, when I went in for a CT scan and MRI, doctors discovered two lesions in my liver, indicating that I may also have liver cancer.

That got my attention. For people diagnosed with liver cancer at an early stage, the five-year relative survival rate is 36 percent. However, if the cancer has spread, the five-year relative survival rate is 13 percent.[1] Follow-up tests indicated I did *not* have liver cancer.

Our immediate concern was to choose the most effective prostate cancer treatment: active surveillance (regular blood tests, rectal exams, and prostate biopsies), radiation to kill the cancer cells, or surgery to remove the prostate?

We did not want active surveillance. Why allow time for the cancer to grow? While radiation and surgery can be equally effective, we chose surgery. We felt more comfortable knowing that the cancerous growth was completely out of my body. The operation was successful, and on December 19, my doctor called on his way home to say the cancer was gone and that he expected me to do extremely well.

During my month-long recovery, Claire showered me with love. She took care of my every need, including keeping the fireplace burning where I sat, napped, and read, and where we sat together for drinks and quiet talks. Before the surgery, we had decorated the tree and house. The Christmas atmosphere added to our sense of joy and gratitude. There was something unexpectedly tender about being in a state of physical dependence on Claire. I wouldn't have anticipated that my illness would have drawn us closer, but it did.

On Christmas Eve, I wrote a letter to Claire and placed it under the tree.

December 24, 1997
Dearest Claire,

Though I can't go Christmas shopping at the malls, I have been shopping in my mind for presents I want to give you. Some I can give easily, and it's just a matter of arranging for you to have them. Some will take longer to "find," and maybe I'll have to give them to you over the rest of our lifetime; more and more each year, I hope.

The easy gifts are ones that I know you've wanted, and you and I can pick them out as soon as I am driving again. They are:

Cable TV (We'll check the library to learn which is the best).

Paints and easel (There's that good store in D.C. we can go to).

Cellular phone (We'll check the library).

Car coat (London Fog, like mine).

Windows washed (As soon as spring comes).

Furnace cleaned.

Trip to Europe (In spring, summer or fall).

The ones I most want to give you will be the ones I want to give for the rest of our lifetime, more and more each year.

They are to listen more, and be less defensive. Probably it all comes down to listening and hearing what you are saying to me. This is the biggest gift I want to give you. It would also be a gift to me, because everything you say to me, you say out of love. So, if I listen, I will hear you saying things to me that you say because you love me.

My other gift is to tell you that I love you, and am grateful for how much you love me. My life has been so rich since we met. You've brought out of me an ability to be honest and to deal with things as they come along. I still tend to want to push unpleasant things aside—but not so much as I used to, thanks to you.

I am grateful for the elegant, peaceful and enjoyable home you have created in each house we have had in our twenty-seven years.

Most of all, I am grateful for you, for who you are, for your passionate honesty, your intelligence, your friendship and love, your sense of humor, your love and knowledge of art, and above all, your spirit.

I love you, Claire, and I want you to have joy and peace today (Christmas) and joy, joy and peace every remaining day of your life.

All my love,
Jim

Part V

In My Inmost Being,

You Teach Me Wisdom

24

I returned to work in February, and we opened the pool in May. Claire, working from home, did laps twice a day. These normal activities felt precious in the aftermath of my illness. We planned to take a long vacation the following summer—perhaps return to Italy.

But that fall, Claire began to feel exhausted. She felt pain in her shoulders and back when she tried to roll over in bed. And she had difficulty getting out of bed. The top of her head and temples were tender to the touch. Tylenol eased the pain, but only partially. By December, the pain had spread to her jaws, and she had stopped eating.

Her primary care physician made an appointment with a rheumatologist, who saw her three times in eight weeks. Each time, he took blood tests to determine the level of inflammation in her system, measured as the sedimentation rate (sed rate).[1] Two days after her third test, he called to say her sed rate was 125, four times the normal rate for females. He ordered biopsies of her temporal arteries for the following morning.

Immediately after the biopsies, he called to say, "Mrs. Callahan, the biopsies indicate that you have giant cell temporal arteritis, a rare and potentially dangerous autoimmune disease.[2] You likely also have polymyalgia rheumatica."[3]

The immediate danger was that the arteritis would restrict the flow of blood from her temporal arteries to her optic nerve and cause blindness. He prescribed fifty milligrams of prednisone a day, and told her he had made an appointment for the following day with a neuro-ophthalmologist.

The doctor's emphasis on "potentially dangerous" and "blindness" was devastating. Claire took the first dose of prednisone that afternoon.

After the second day on prednisone, she was pain-free. She looked at me from the top of the stairs, arms raised in a victory salute, and told me how much better she felt. Relief! A physician friend with whom I shared the news said, "She probably feels like she could walk to New York."

The neuro-ophthalmologist found no damage to the optic nerve. Her sed rate fell to the normal range. We felt she was out of the woods. But it soon rose again, and her prednisone was increased to eighty milligrams a day.

After a year on a high dose of prednisone, Claire's sed rate returned to normal, and the medication was discontinued. But it had taken a toll on her body. By fall, her legs and feet began to swell. The muscles in her legs became rigid. She lost the feeling in her toes and the soles of her feet, and could not sense where her feet were. She could not stand for more than twenty minutes. Her exhaustion worsened. She couldn't drive. She needed a walker in the house, and a wheelchair outside the house. She was housebound without my aid.

Claire asked her rheumatologist to refer her to the Mayo Clinic in Rochester, Minnesota, where the foremost researcher on giant cell arteritis, Gene Hunter, M.D., worked. Her doctor was reluctant, saying it would be difficult to make an appointment at Mayo on short notice. Besides, he didn't see much to be gained by going there.

I called Dr. Richard Hurt, at Mayo, an ASAM member and friend, and asked if he could arrange for Claire to be seen. Fifteen minutes later he called to say rheumatologist Steven Ytterberg would see her, and gave me Dr. Ytterberg's number. Dr. Ytterberg's secretary asked, "How soon can she come?"

Our experience at Mayo confirmed its reputation for thoroughness and quality patient care. Claire was examined by several specialists over a three-day period. They confirmed the diagnoses, but were unable to offer hope to halt the progression of the disorders caused by the prednisone, or reverse their symptoms. They did make useful suggestions for managing the symptoms, such as wrapping her legs each day to keep the swelling in check.

Claire was seventy-one; I was sixty-two. We'd both looked forward to an active retirement, with travel, volunteer work, and visits with friends, but those dreams were slipping away. Instead, Claire's disability defined our lives. We frequently discussed her illness and how we needed to adjust our lives to it.

On a snowy evening in November 2001, one such conversation marked a turning point in our lives. We were in the den. Claire was in the easy chair where she now spent most of her time, and I was kneeling on the floor in front of her, holding her hands as she cried. I softly asked, "What do you want to do, love?" She began to sob. "I want to go home!"

I said, "We will."

Whenever, in earlier years, Claire and I talked about retirement, we spoke of Austin, or North Carolina, or Atlanta. We never spoke of retiring to Danvers. After she had passed away, I found this in her papers:

> *In the few streets or fields of your childhood,*
> *There, no matter how widely you travel,*
> *You will live and die.*4

Claire was eager to live close to her brothers, Joe and John, and their wives, Joan and Liz, as well as her nephews and nieces and their husbands and children. She wanted to be near the remaining friends she had known as a girl, and the "few streets and fields of (her) childhood."

It was not a question of, "What do you mean?" Or "Is that really what you want?" Or "I'm not ready to retire." It was a matter of what steps do we now take to resign from my position, put our house on the market, and find a home in or near Danvers. Claire had so often put her wishes aside to accommodate me. It was time for me to do what Claire wanted.

The next morning, I called ASAM President Dr. Anne Geller to tell her of Claire's condition and my decision to resign, effective June 30. I told her I would commute from Boston to D.C. each week until the search committee had located my replacement.

We put our house on the market and flew to Boston to visit neighborhoods in Danvers and nearby towns. We settled on Danvers and Topsfield as preferred locations. Claire made note of the streets that most appealed to her. Parsonage Lane in Topsfield was on her list. In late December, 22 Parsonage came on the market. Our offer was accepted.

IN MY INMOST BEING, YOU TEACH ME WISDOM

Our friends John and Annie Hisle hosted a going-away dinner. It was a joy to be with friends and fellow Holy Trinity parishioners. Their love had sustained us when we lived in D.C., and they promised their prayers and continued support after we moved.

While Claire looked forward to sharing her siblings' lives more fully, we both grieved the end of the present chapter of our lives. We would be leaving close friends, a parish that fed our faith, and a Washington community we had enjoyed.

I had to make adjustments in my emotions and professional plans. I wasn't ready to retire; not ready to end my professional career. My leaving might put the achievement of ABMS recognition in jeopardy. I had reason to be anxious about whether—after I was gone—the new director and board would finish the work and gain recognition.

Claire understood this, and we agreed that, once I had completed the commutes to Washington and retired in July from full-time work, I would work part-time from home.

From 2002 to 2008 I worked under contract with ASAM to develop state medical specialty societies (SMSSs) of addiction medicine, ASAM chapters. The goal was to build a national network to advocate for recognition of addiction medicine. Dr. Rick Beach and then Dr. Kevin Kunz chaired the program. Program participants were the SMSS chapter presidents. I was away from home overnight three or four times a year, one night each time. A family member stayed with Claire.

In 2008, our SMSS work completed, we formed the American Board of Addiction Medicine (ABAM) and the ABAM Foundation to certify physicians in addiction medicine and to comply with ABMS requirements. I agreed to be ABAM and

ABAM Foundation executive vice president. The board of directors agreed that I would work part-time.

Kevin Kunz, the ABAM president, lived in Hawaii, a five-hour time difference; so my evening hours were his prime daylight hours to work with me. That meant Claire and I could spend most days together, and I could work evenings in my office.

We spent many mornings or afternoons at John and Liz's kitchen table, where Claire, John, and Liz would reminisce about Danvers and the 'Port. On Sunday afternoons, we'd watch Tom Brady and the Patriots, which often, for John, was more agony than enjoyment. He cringed when the team fell behind or when Coach Belichick called "a stupid play."

Claire's condition worsened. She couldn't walk or exercise enough to control her weight, and went from 145 to 235 pounds, from a size twelve dress to a twenty-four. Her feet swelled so much she could no longer wear shoes, and had to rely on heavy cotton socks. Her legs began to ooze lymph and become infected. They itched, became hot, and were sensitive to any touch, even by the bedsheets. So she slept in a recliner with cold packs on her legs. Steam would rise when I placed them on her skin, and she would sigh with relief.

Conditions from earlier, "milder" illnesses aggravated Claire's increasing disability and discomfort. The mitral valve prolapse she had had since the early 1970s, and the atrial fibrillation from the late 1980s, worsened. She became depressed. Acid reflux became a problem. Her vision was poor. When she read, watched TV, or looked at an object or person, there were "floaters," like cobwebs or dust in her field of vision. Coupled with the "floaters" was a blurred and distorted central vision, the result of surface wrinkling retinopathy, or macular pucker.

To escape the confines of the house and the constant focus on these torments, we would take short trips to Maine.

Kittery, Maine is known for its outlet stores. We'd load the wheelchair into the trunk, drive the pleasant forty miles up I-95, spend a couple of hours navigating the shops' narrow aisles, have lunch, and be home before dark. An enjoyable day.

Portland is a longer drive, ninety miles. We'd stay at the South Portland Marriott. It was always a special treat for Claire that I had concierge floor privileges from the many conferences ASAM sponsored at Marriott hotels. We'd reserve a corner room, and in the morning, I would bring a tray for breakfast in bed.

We could then visit the Portland Museum of Art, or, if she was up to a longer drive home, we would go to Freeport for LL Bean and the boutique clothing and art stores.

A special treat was a visit to Goose Rocks Beach, Kennebunkport, Maine, one of the few sandy beaches in the state. The wheelchair would get us close enough that she could walk the short distance to a beach chair and umbrella. On one occasion, we looked at ocean-front rental cottages.

We found a cottage with a one-step-down access to the beach. It had five bedrooms and rented for $15,000 a month. Claire said, "Totally out of the question. Absolutely not. Never. Ridiculous." I said, "Claire, the price is ridiculous, but we have no children who need our support, no outstanding obligations.

"This would be a luxury for you at this time of your life when you have been so sick. We can invite John and Liz to stay with us, Ralph and Donna, and your other nieces and nephews and their families. Why not?" Claire said, "Because it's wrong for someone to ask that kind of money to rent a cottage; that's why."

Claire often denied herself things she wanted, because she felt the price was unjust. She would have felt uncomfortable for the entire month if she knew we'd paid $15,000. In retrospect, I should have rented it and told her we paid $3,000! I wish I had.

Our longest side trip was to Bar Harbor and Acadia National Park, Maine. It was offseason, and easier to get around by wheelchair. On our drive through the park I came eye to eye with a large antlered buck deer. We rounded a bend just as the deer was about to cross the road. He leaned into my driver-side door, gently denting it, and only my car door window separated his large, wild eye and my small, nervous eye. We looked at each other for an instant before he bolted back to the woods.

Our favorite local drive was Route 127, the coast road to Gloucester.

Our ride had a rhythm. Topsfield to Route 62 in Beverly, past the Beverly Public Library (Claire: "Fran Cassey's father was the Library censor."), down Dane Street to Dane Street Beach (Claire: "This is where I first became a Red Cross lifeguard. I received my certification when I was seventeen."), to 127 past Endicott College, into Beverly Farms and past stone and brick mansions that lined the coast and walled off the sea from view (Claire: "The wealthy Boston Brahmans had their summer homes in Beverly Farms; their chauffeurs would drive to the station to meet them."). Then past the railroad station to West Beach where we'd enjoy the view of the Atlantic (Claire: "I was Red Cross lifeguard here too").

From there we'd go to Manchester-by-the-Sea (Jim: "Would you like to stop at the used bookstore?" Claire: "Yes, that would be nice."). After browsing, we'd drive past Captain Dusty's Ice

IN MY INMOST BEING, YOU TEACH ME WISDOM

Cream to Manchester Harbor and white yachts with blue sail covers that signal relaxation and peace.

Then to Magnolia, past the Manchester Bath and Tennis Club (Jim: "My ASAM friend, Dr. Dan McCullough is a member; he'd be happy to sponsor our membership." Claire: "I don't think so.") into Magnolia where there is a small one- or two-car pullover and an open view of the Atlantic (Claire; "Ireland is just out there."). We'd talk quietly for a while (Jim: "I think I'll take a nap.") and I'd put my seat in recline and sleep for half an hour, while Claire gazed across the ocean. I never asked what she thought of during those private moments.

(Jim: "Would you like some clam chowder?" Claire: "I'd love some.") Back onto 127 to Gloucester, a left on 133 to the Causeway Restaurant; Italian. Specialties? Seafood. We'd park across the street in sight of Gloucester High School, and I'd go to the Causeway. Small (ten tables) and noisy; fresh seafood, and the best Clam "Chowdah" in New England. I'd work my way to the register, past the crowd waiting for a table. "Two bowls of Clam to go, extra bread and butter." The Chowder was always hot, and the Italian bread fresh.

Home by 133 to 128 South. Spring and summer we'd stop in Danvers at the Cherry Farm Creamery. (Jim: What kind of ice cream would you like?" Claire: "Strawberry." Jim: "I think I'll get Moose Trax.")

Then a short ride home on route 97.

Treasured memories.

It meant something to me to act as Claire's chauffeur. I couldn't do much to alleviate her pain, but I could help her experience these small delights. I could express my love through a hundred small acts of service.

25

One night, shortly after moving to Topsfield, we turned on the evening news and were startled to see a man in handcuffs—a Rev. John Geoghan—being arraigned on charges of child sexual abuse. He was one of several priests in the Boston Archdiocese charged with sexual molestation of children. The *Boston Globe* Spotlight Team brought this issue to the attention of the whole country.

After the *Globe* exposé, some Catholics began to meet for "listening sessions" in parish halls, and express anger and grief at the priests' abuses and cover-ups by the hierarchy.

Parishioners in Wellesley, Massachusetts, formed the Voice of the Faithful (VOTF), a watchdog group to promote the participation of lay Catholics in the governance and guidance of the Church.[1]

Two members of our Topsfield Saint Rose of Lima parish, Dr. Vince and Jolene Guerra, organized a VOTF chapter. Claire was an ardent supporter and attended meetings where she spoke of the need to hold the clergy and hierarchy accountable.

Eight years after we'd watched John Geoghan's arraignment, Claire read a story in the *Globe* about a parochial grade school that had refused to admit a child whose parents were lesbian. Archbishop Sean O'Malley had intervened to place the child in a different parochial school, and the *Globe* reported this as an example of the Church making amends for the first school's failure to admit the child. Claire wrote a letter to the editor to take exception to the *Globe* naming this "making amends." The caption to her letter read, "Another case of child abuse."

May 19, 2010

A GLARING omission in your May 14 editorial, "After Hingham school errs, archdiocese makes amends," is that perpetrators of child abuse have once again not been held accountable by the Archdiocese of Boston.

We sadly remember Cardinal Law's practice of transferring from parish-to-parish priests who sexually abused children, rather than dealing directly with the problem by removing the abusing priests from the ministry and holding them accountable.

Now, Cardinal O'Malley, who has jurisdiction over Saint Paul's Catholic elementary school in Hingham, failed to exercise his authority to address, with the parish pastor and school principal, the grave injustice against an 8-year-old boy whose admission to the school was rescinded because his parents are lesbian.

Rather than address the root of the problem by removing the pastor and principal, or by requiring that they adhere to the archdiocesan (and Gospel) policy of nondiscrimination, the archdiocese will help find a new Catholic school for the boy.

The child is identified as the problem, and is shifted to another school. And the real problems, the discriminating pastor and principal, are allowed to remain in their positions, and perhaps continue to discriminate. This gives tacit approval to the parish and school policy.

The child is not the cause of the problem; he is the victim.
Claire Callahan,

Topsfield © Copyright 2010 Globe Newspaper Company.

A few months later, she wrote in response to the Archdiocese of Boston campaign to "recruit" Catholics who no longer came to Mass or other church services—people often spoken of as "fallen away Catholics." The campaign was "A call to Catholics to 'come home' again." The *Globe* editorial staff's caption above Claire's letter was, "Church's invitation engraved with hypocrisy."

July 25, 2010

Would you accept an invitation to "come home" again, if, as a woman, you were regarded as only a partial member of the family, and one for whom advocating women's ordination to the priesthood is described as a grave sin in the same category as pedophilia?

Would you "come home" again, if there were a "funny uncle" protected by the head of your family, at your children's peril?

Would you "come home" again if you were gay or lesbian, and knew that the "family" does not accept you, or may not admit your child to a parochial school?

People will come home again in countless numbers when

IN MY INMOST BEING, YOU TEACH ME WISDOM

the leaders of the family embody in their behavior the message of the family founder: "Come to me, all you who labor and are overburdened, and I will give you rest."

Public-relations media blitzes and blogs are no match for Christ's words that sustain my faith.

Claire Callahan, Topsfield

© Copyright 2010 Globe Newspaper Company.

When I read Claire's words, I can hear the little girl standing up to her father's violence, the teenager determined to get to college, the teacher who fought for her students, and the woman who chose to follow her conscience even when it meant risking her friends' and family's disapproval. Though her body was weak, Claire was still finding ways to devote herself to the service of others.

I RETIRED IN DECEMBER 2012. While we did spend our days together, I found myself unwilling to spend the evenings with her. I felt fidgety. I needed to tackle a project, get something done. I had an itch to work and be useful the way I'd been for most of my career.

I'd say, "I'm going to work upstairs a while." Claire would say, "Please stay." I'd tell her I wouldn't be long. But sometimes it *was* long—two or three hours.

This pattern persisted for a couple of years. I mostly turned a deaf ear to Claire's pleas, justifying my absence by saying that I needed to work. I've had waves of guilt and regret for not spending those evenings with Claire. The truth is, those evening hours in my office helped me cope.

She went to the Beverly Hospital Emergency Department, or was admitted to the hospital, ten times from 2007 to her passing in 2016. She kept a suitcase packed, in case we had to go to the hospital in the middle of the night. In April 2015, she spent twelve days in the hospital with severe edema. She was filled with water: feet, ankles, legs, bowels, lungs.

After discharge, we set up a hospital bed in our library, but she didn't use it. She spent her days and nights in the recliner. I moved my bed into the room, and I turned the dining room into the "medical supply center."

Visiting nurses came three times a week to treat and dress her wounds and wrap her legs. I continued to wrap on the other days. Only gradually did I learn that other types of home health care were available to help bathe Claire and wash her hair, trim her toenails.

One such gentle woman, Catherine Smith, took a book of garden flowers from the shelf and, for an hour, walked with Claire through the beautiful pages. When Claire passed, she visited the funeral home website and wrote, "Claire, I was honored to care for you during your illness. I wish I had more time with you. I will miss your beautiful smile and conversation."

I continued to prepare her meals, slipping in a treat of her favorite German chocolate cake or other sweet, or finding a flower to put on her tray.

Her brother John, and her nieces Donna and Nancy, would spell me, so that I could go food shopping, or go to Macy's for a nightgown or underwear for Claire. At first, I felt self-conscious sorting through the panties for the correct size in all cotton, or checking out the bras. But I got used to it, and so did the saleswomen. I paid no attention to the women shoppers trying not to let me know they were eyeing me.

I would kneel in front of Claire in the recliner, put my arms on her legs and say, "I'm sorry you have to suffer like this." She would put her hand on my head and say, "I'm sorry I am putting you through this." Sometimes it seemed like all we could do was feel the pain together.

During this time, she showed the first signs of dementia.

This complicated her life. She could no longer read a novel, or follow a TV program, or track a story I read to her. She had full mental capacities for the present conversation and full comprehension of what was occurring. But, once the incident passed, it was gone from her memory. This led to unexpectedly endearing moments.

One night, we went to bed around 2 a.m. The lights were out, and Claire was in her recliner, covered with a blanket, her feet elevated on the hassock. It was time to sleep, but Claire kept talking. From my bed nearby, I responded with short answers, spoken softly, hoping this would encourage her to sleep. Instead, she kept talking. This went on for about thirty minutes. I said, "Love, if we don't sleep, I won't be awake enough tomorrow to help you. Can we go to sleep?" But it had no effect.

Finally, I said, "Love, I'm going to have to go upstairs to sleep. If I don't, I won't be able to help you tomorrow." In exasperation she said, "Oh, go upstairs then!"

I gathered my pillow and blanket and went upstairs. At seven in the morning, I heard Claire calling. When I walked into the library, I saw that she had somehow gotten out of her recliner and was sitting on the hassock. I expected her to point at my empty bed and say, "Where have you been, you son of a bitch?" Instead, she looked at me with a beaming smile and said, "You found me!"

Several years earlier she told me she dreamt she was lost, but knew I would come to find her. Now, Claire's smile melted my heart. In that moment, I could see her—really see her, the way I had when we'd first fallen in love. The thick veil Claire's illness had thrown over her fell away, and there she was. I wanted to keep her in that moment, to freeze her there before her suffering dragged her back under. I took her hand and smiled back.

26

On February 3, 2016, Claire's doctor, Hugh Taylor, made "a home visit." He told me the fluid build-up in her body was severe, and her congestive heart failure was advanced. He didn't think she had long to live, and told me he would do the necessary paperwork to have her admitted to Kaplan Family Hospice House.

After he left, I knelt in front of Claire, with my hands in hers. She said, "I'm very sick, aren't I?" I said, "You're dying, love." She answered, "Does my mother know?" I said, "I'm not certain, but I think she does."

Claire had never been afraid of death. As a Sister of the Holy Cross, she'd observed a monthly day of silence, prayer, and meditation during which she did an hour of reflection on the mystery of death—including her own. Several years earlier, she'd written her obituary, and had prepared the liturgy for her funeral Mass.

She had what Cornel West, grandson of a Baptist minister, calls "thick" faith.[1] She didn't talk much about her faith, or take part in prayer groups or Bible study groups. She lived Jesus' teaching, "Love one another," in a straightforward way; what my friend Kevin Kunz calls "lived faith."

Even during Claire's hospital stays, her focus was on the doctors, nurses, aides, cleaning staff, and meal-service staff. She was always asking, "How long have you been doing this? Do you enjoy your work? Do you have a family?" She would never fail to ask the young nurses' aides, "Are you thinking of getting your RN?"

One evening, as I was kneeling in front of her chair, my hands on her knees, Claire said softly, "He must trust me, to give me this."

She said it almost to herself. She wasn't looking at me, or speaking to me. We hadn't been talking. It was as though a private thought had escaped her mind. At that moment, Claire opened to me a window onto her inner self and her relationship with God. He (God) trusted (loved) her, and gave her this (suffering). It was the same window Jesus opened to his disciples on the night of his betrayal, when he fell to the ground and prayed that, if it were possible, the hour would pass from Him.

Although Jesus struggled to understand how his Father could want him to accept suffering, he knew his Father loved him, and that the suffering would somehow turn to good. The same was true for Claire. I was struck by how matter of fact, yet how momentous, her statement was.

I looked at the plain wooden cross she was wearing. I knew when she said, "He must trust me, to give me this," that the "this" was her suffering, her cross. The cross was central to Claire's understanding of her Christian life. On her bedside table, she kept a cross that came with us on vacations, business trips, and hospital stays. A Celtic cross we had bought in Ireland hung in our front hall. When she'd been well enough to move around, she would put her fingers to her lips and then to the cross every morning.

The crosses in our home were Claire's reminders that she, like every person, was going through her share of suffering. They were also a symbol of hope that this suffering would lead to resurrection: *Yet what we suffer now is nothing compared to the glory he will reveal to us later.*[2] Claire never complained about her illness, or said, "Why me? Why does God do this to me?" Instead, she said, "God must trust me, to give me this."

I knew Claire was frustrated that she didn't have the health to be productive for others. I also knew, however, that she'd increasingly turned her suffering into a constant prayer of acceptance of this as her cross. Her last years were not "unproductive" at all—they were years of prayer for others, especially "those who have no one."

That night was Claire's last at our home on Parsonage Lane. I took extra care in tucking in her blankets before she went to sleep. Lying on my own bed close to her recliner, I listened to her breathing. Claire had accepted her death, which she knew to be a reunion with her Abba.

27

The following afternoon, an ambulance came to take Claire to hospice. I drove separately, immediately regretting my decision to drive instead of riding with Claire. Her niece Donna rode with her. This was the last ride Claire would take—the last time she would leave our home—the last everything. At the hospice, I parked the car and hurried out front to meet the ambulance.

For the next seven days, I stayed by Claire's side at Kaplan House, sleeping next to her bed in a recliner. Her brother John came for long visits each day, as well as her nieces, Donna and Nancy. John sat at the foot of her bed, directly in her line of sight.

Fellow St. Rose parishioner, Charlotte O'Toole, brought the Eucharist every day. On Saturday, February 6, Claire's family and Charlotte gathered in Claire's room: her brother and me, her nieces (Mary, Donna, Debbie and Nancy Lyons) and their husbands, her nephew John Lyons and great-nephew Anthony Panciocco and his fiancée Julie Trask. Helen (Brown) and Carl DeCotis and other friends were there. We sang hymns and all received Communion.

February 10 was Ash Wednesday. Our neighbor and friend, Ella Gutowski, brought Claire the ashes and sang to her. By late that afternoon, she was no longer able to speak, and had fallen into a peaceful sleep. I attended to her every breath, her hand in mine.

The next morning, February 11, John came. We stood and sat at Claire's bed, watching her breathing.

At 11:40 a.m., Claire stopped breathing. I turned to John and said, "She's gone."

Within a few minutes, a nurse came to confirm Claire's passing. Helen and Carl had come to visit; it was Helen's birthday. Donna and Helen prepared Claire's body. As the funeral director wheeled her body past me, I whispered to myself, "Tell me where you are, and I will come to find you!"

The next day, I was driving when I felt a surge of joy at knowing that Claire was with God. I began to sing Handel's Hallelujah Chorus. When I got home, I called the parish music director to ask that she play it at Claire's Mass. She gently reminded me that it was Lent, and we don't sing Hallelujah at Mass in Lent.

It was a tribute to Claire and her family, especially John, that, despite the freezing weather and the icy road and sidewalk conditions, many elderly friends from the 'Port paid their respects at Claire's wake. Guest after guest clasped my hand and told me how much Claire meant to them, or shared a memory from their childhoods.

I was consoled by my family and friends who joined with the members of Claire's family to express their condolences. My nephews (Jim, Kevin, and Brian Laughlin) and cousins (Peg Scott Darrah and Marilyn Scott) came. As did friends: Ann Pitra

IN MY INMOST BEING, YOU TEACH ME WISDOM

and her daughter Sarah Sorenson, Kevin Kunz, and my friend since freshman high school, Tom Norris, and friends from the Voice of the Faithful, parishioners, and neighborhood friends.

Donna and Ralph hosted a reception for family and out-of-town guests. Tom Norris stayed at my house for several days. We spent the first night talking and sipping Jameson Irish Whiskey.

At the Mass, Donna spoke for the family. I also spoke—of Claire's love of her family, her empathy for the needy, her faith, and how she challenged church leaders to live Jesus' gospel of love.

IN THE DAYS following the burial, I was grateful that I had pressing tasks to deal with. This kept grief at bay. I called the medical supply company to remove the oxygen tanks, oxygen concentrator, wheelchair, as well as the hospital bed that had sat, unused, beside the recliner where Claire had slept for eleven months. I busied myself with sending thank-you notes to the family, friends, and neighbors who had assisted Claire in her illness, came to the wake or Mass, sent Mass or condolence cards and emails, or sent flowers or brought food.

Donna disposed of the medical supplies and medications that filled the dining room and kitchen tables. I couldn't bring myself to do this. I folded, boxed, and donated her clothing. (I didn't immediately get rid of all her clothing. The irrational thought was that she might need some!) I sent thank-you letters and donations to the Topsfield Fire and Rescue Department, Care Dimensions, and Fr. Medas, and letters to Dr. Taylor and his office staff, and the director of Kaplan Family Hospice. I removed Claire's name from accounts, notified Social Security, settled her estate and estate taxes.

These tasks were painful. It was as though I was repeatedly and officially pronouncing Claire dead.

But as hard as I tried to keep it away, grief began to make its presence known. I could feel it like an approaching storm cloud, gray and heavy.

I gradually had to face the reality of life without Claire. In the absence of any work or responsibilities, I found myself adrift. I realized I needed a routine to prop me up. As a starting point, I decided to say "yes" to all invitations, as well as to all requests for assistance. I would also go to bed at a more reasonable hour and get up early for weekday Masses. Evenings? I was not a TV watcher. I decided to systematically read our collection of art books. The house? Every Saturday, do the laundry and clean the bathrooms and one or two rooms. This would ensure the whole house got cleaned every six or seven weeks!

I was trying to set up barriers against grief. But grief seeped through my barriers. My emotions confused me. Claire was with God in eternal joy—so why did I feel so sad? Why did I feel like half of me had died?

When I'd walk in the front door, I'd call out to Claire as I always had: "I'm home, Claire." Calling her name eased the pain. I understood what Dante meant:

> *I am not what I am,*
> *And so my shame drives me away from others;*
> *And then I weep alone in my lamenting,*
> *Calling to Beatrice, "Can you be dead?"*
> *And just to call her name restores my soul.*[1]

IN MY INMOST BEING, YOU TEACH ME WISDOM

Although I put up a good show for neighbors and acquaintances, my sorrow poured out in tears and sobs when I was alone or with a close friend. In a letter of condolence, one of Claire's former students wrote, "Your loss must be tremendous, and I pray that it doesn't engulf you."

Engulf! She understood. Grief nearly did engulf me—and might have, had I not had the support of family, friends, and the Hospice bereavement groups.

Often, a family member and two close friends sat with me or listened on the phone for hours as I confessed, in tears, my guilt at not having loved Claire enough. I couldn't get the guilt out of my system. It was lodged inside me like a stone. There was no knocking it loose, and I wondered if I would live with its pain for the rest of my life.

Friends encouraged me to join a support group and so, three weeks after Claire passed away, I attended an open session at the Bertolon Center (Kaplan House) for people who had lost a loved one. About thirty people came. Some sat and listened. Others spoke, quietly or in tears, of spouses, infants and young children, parents, siblings, and friends who had died. Often, as a person spoke, the person sitting next to her, a stranger, would quietly place her hand on the person's arm, or move the box of tissues closer.

I was so absorbed by the stories, and the extent of the sorrow in the room, that I was unaware of the traffic passing by the windows. Thanks to that session, I woke up to the danger of getting lost in myself, and forgetting that I was only one of millions of people mourning the death of a loved one. At the end of the session, I signed up for a Loss of Spouse/Partner bereavement group.

The group was seven women and three men. All of us had been married for at least forty years; one or two of us, for more than fifty. The facilitator was a soft-spoken and congenial lay volunteer whose wife had passed away several years earlier. He introduced himself and spoke of his wife's illness and death. He understood.

At each session, we spoke openly. Honestly. No one was forced to share. Although none of us had met before, we spoke as though to friends whom we had known for years. The experience was profound. As one participant said, "We clung to each other. It was truth-telling." We met eight times at the Bertolon Center, and continued meeting at my house, monthly, for another year.

I read every article or book listed in the bereavement resource packet. The books I found particularly helpful were by authors who had lost a spouse: C.S. Lewis' *A Grief Observed*, and Joan Didion's *The Year of Magical Thinking*.

Lewis spoke of the inadequacy of his faith to comfort him at this most painful moment. He wrote, "Talk to me about the truth of religion, and I will listen gladly. Talk to me about the duty of religion and I will listen submissively. But don't come talking to me about the consolations of religion or I shall suspect that you don't understand."[2]

Joan Didion spoke of her hesitancy to discard her husband's shoes, thinking that he might need them.[3] It helped me to know that I wasn't the only person to have these strange thoughts, or to feel these waves of regret, longing, and inconsolable sadness.

My greatest sorrow was to realize how completely Claire had loved me, and how often I had failed to love her. Indeed, her love was a gift that I only began to understand after she passed away. In this, I felt a kinship with Augustine, who wrote about his love of God:

> *Late have I loved you,*
> *Beauty so ancient and so new,*
> *late have I loved you!* 4

Claire admired me, encouraged me, consoled me, challenged me. Her love transformed me. When I described this to a friend, she replied, "I've never been loved like that!"

My greatest sorrow, in my grief, was the realization of how completely she loved me, and how often I failed to love her.

Three weeks after her passing, I found a note pinned to the first page of her address book:

"As you know so well, the passage of time never really heals the tragic memory of such a great loss, but we carry on, because we have to, because our loved ones would want us to, and because there is still light to guide us in the world from the love they gave us."

Senator Ted Kennedy wrote the above words to a widow of a man killed in the September 11, 2001 World Trade Center terrorist attack. President Obama cited these words when delivering the eulogy for Senator Kennedy on August 29, 2009 at Our Lady of Perpetual Help Basilica, Roxbury, Massachusetts.

It comforts me to think that Claire may have clipped this to her address book so that I might find it when looking for addresses of those to notify of her passing.

28

Support of family and friends as well as the bereavement group sessions were comforting. The routine I had constructed kept me active, but would I spend the rest of my life in grief and in routines created to contain it?

Should I go back to work as a consultant with my former organization? I attended a planning session on strategies to establish addiction medicine training fellowships.[1] Ted Tschudy, a friend and former colleague, facilitated the meetings.

As Kevin Kunz, Ted, and I reviewed the meeting outcomes and next steps, Kevin invited me to return to work part-time. I said, "Kevin, as grateful as I am that you've asked me, I can't see myself returning to work. I feel as though I have one leg in time and one in eternity."

Ted said, "You're on a journey."

"On a journey." Seeking, searching. No destination. But, yes, on a journey. When Claire passed away, I stepped, unawares, into a new existence. One leg in time with familiar surroundings; one in eternity, with Claire.

During my 1964 pastoral year at Notre Dame I attended a class by Fr. John Dunne. In his autobiography, *A Journey with*

God in Time,[2] he writes, "Life is about learning to love . . . and about the learning that comes of loving,"[3] and coming to realize that, in life, we are on "a journey with God in time . . . a companionship with God in love and death."[4] . . . We do not simply choose; we discover our way in life."[5] And on our life's journey we learn that:

> *Things are meant;*
> *There are signs;*
> *The heart speaks;*
> *There is a way.*[6]

What John wrote has unfolded for me in ways I had not planned or envisioned.

In April, Jim McDonough invited me to Austin. I hadn't been there in years and was eager to see Jim, visit some of my and Claire's favorite places, and spend time with friends.

Jim is warm and welcoming. A quiet voice that gives no hint of the strength of his convictions and steely common sense. He knows how to listen, to offer a thought rather than a precept. He loves.

The others I wanted to see were our friend and Claire's maid of honor, Karen Bordelon Hartwell, and our friends George and Alice Richards Pryor. George had been a Dominican priest with Jim McDonough at Saint Edward's. Alice taught art at UT. I also wanted to visit Carmon Koile, the wife of our UT professor, Earl Koile, who had passed away in 2013.

During our first morning together, Jim and I sat and talked for a long time at the breakfast table. I'd cry at a painful memory, then laugh when I recalled some wonderful moment with Claire. I told him of my regrets, my guilt, and my shame at not spending as much time with Claire as I could have. At the end of our conversation, I knelt and asked for absolution. It was the first time I'd been to confession in thirty years.

The next day I visited Carmon Koile. We had never met. I brought flowers and chocolates. I expressed my condolences. I told her I had come as a tribute to Earl; that he had affected my life and Claire's in important ways. I thanked her for supporting Earl's work during their sixty-five years of marriage. "From my personal life," I said, "I know how much a wife contributes to a husband's success, and how little it is recognized." We visited Earl's grave.

I toured the UT campus, stopped by the buildings where Claire and I had most of our classes, went to lunch at the Texas Exes (alumni) club, visited the Catholic Student Center where we were married, and walked a couple of blocks on The Drag, the section of Guadalupe Street that runs along the western edge of the campus.

I walked the grounds of the Texas Capitol, visited the Travis County Courthouse where Claire had worked as a probation officer, and took photos of the courthouse and a deputy sheriff who was interested to hear of Claire's work there.

I then drove to the neighborhood where Claire had her first apartment on Crockett Street in South Austin, walked the University of Saint Edward's campus, and sat for a while at the building where we first met.

Karen and Ed came to Jim's for dinner, and we reminisced.

On my last day, Jim drove me to the site of the former Travis State School.[7] I found my way to the cemetery. The grave markers are flat stones.[8] Some have no name; some have only a first or last name. Some have only a name and no dates. Some are blank. I prayed in gratitude for these beautiful and mostly forgotten men with whom Claire and I had shared so many hours of joy.

It was time to come back to Boston. Jim and I were standing beside his car at the check-in lane. I pulled my suitcase from the trunk and put it beside me to give him a hug. He put his hands on the sides of my shoulders, drew me close, and kissed me on the cheek.

A MONTH after Claire passed away, I began to write letters to her. They were in the form of a conversation. I called them "Dialogues." In our first, March 30, I wrote, "I call these entries Dialogues. You speak to me in a way that only my heart can hear." Each ended, "I love you, Claire. I love you too, Jim."

Was I living a fantasy? Was I creating a make-believe world? Was I getting goofy?

No. If what Catholics pray at a funeral Mass is true, *For your faithful, Lord, life is changed, not ended*,[9] then Claire lives. And, if the Christian belief in the "Communion of Saints" is true, then those who have passed and those in time commune. Not in seances and apparitions. Not in internal voices. We commune in love.

Paul wrote, *Love never ends.*[10] *And now these three remain: faith, hope and love, but the greatest of these is love.*[11] *You must want love more than anything else.*[12]

Love never ends, because *God is love.*[13] And God is eternal. No beginning, no end.

It is in the moments when we love that we are in communion with those whose entire existence is love, with those who live in eternal love. If Claire lives, and if Claire communes, then she lives and communes in love. And that is where I will hear her speak to me. When I love in the course of my day-to-day life, Claire and I are in dialogue.

On July 8, at morning Mass, Psalm 51 read, *[I]n my inmost being, you teach me wisdom.* In the letter that day, I wrote, "You are leading me to places within myself where I have never been. You teach me wisdom."

I dreamt of Claire twice: once on Friday, April 29, and again on Monday, May 9. In the first dream, Claire returned home after a long trip and came running to embrace me. I was flooded with joy and relief that we were together again.

In the second dream, Claire was standing at the front door of our house, preparing to leave. I called for her to wait, and came down the stairs to embrace her. She was young, and looked just like the high school photo she had asked me to place by her coffin. She was wearing a babushka—a headscarf tied under the chin. I asked her if she was happy, and Claire said, "Yes." Then I said, "And how is Jesus?" Claire smiled and said, "He's great!"

When I woke up, I felt as though a weight had been lifted. Through my dreams, Claire seemed to be telling me, "I am alive. I am happy. Do not mourn. Engage in your life completely."

Were these dreams merely the products of a grief-stricken mind? Or were they extraordinary examples of dialogue between a deceased person in eternity and a living partner in time? I believe these dreams were real encounters—that Claire and I communed with each other, our fingers nearly touching across the threshold of eternity.

IN MY INMOST BEING, YOU TEACH ME WISDOM

LATER THAT SUMMER, I received a newsletter from Mount Saint Mary's Abbey in Wrentham, Massachusetts, home to about forty cloistered Cistercian sisters.[14] Claire and I had first visited the Abbey in the 1970s, and in recent years we'd spent several Christmas Eves and Christmases there. I decided to send a donation, including a note about Claire's illness and passing. I wrote, "A few years ago, we spent our Christmas in your guest rooms attached to the Abbey. I will never forget the warm welcome one of your sisters gave Claire on that occasion. I can still see her embracing Claire."

Five days later, I received a letter from the abbess, Mother Maureen McCabe, in which she prayed that "our Loving Mother will draw [Claire] ever deeper into her own and Jesus' eternal embrace, refreshing and comforting your heart at the inundating springs of her peace and consolation." Her tenderness moved me. I thought, *This woman knows love. I want to meet her.* I made a reservation for a December 24–27 retreat, and requested to meet her.

On the day we met, Mother Maureen wore a white habit, a full-length black scapular held at the waist by a brown leather belt, and a black veil falling to her shoulders. She was about five-foot-five, with great energy and a wonderful smile. She said, "I received your letter and want to express my sorrow over Claire's death. I don't think I met her." We sat and talked for a while, and she told me that she had been a Sister of Mercy and taught high school before entering the Cistercian order.

We began speaking about prayer and Christ. I explained that my prayer principally consisted of reading the scriptures, trying to live them in my daily life, and asking God to teach me to love. I told her of my experience in Rome, when I knew I was one with Jesus in the Garden of Gethsemane, and that God was my Abba, my Father. She told me of her experience, when a Mercy Sister, of God's overwhelming love for her, his tenderness. Then she said, "We've been marked."

It was time for Vespers. I knelt to ask her blessing. She quickly helped me to my feet. "No, no. Please no!" I had unintentionally embarrassed her. Before she left, I said, "May I ask you to be my spiritual director?" She said, "Let's talk some more tomorrow, and then we can discuss that."

We met for another hour the next afternoon. I asked, "Could I come back maybe three or four times a year for a retreat and to speak with you?" She said, "I was thinking the same thing. How about three times a year?" She suggested that I set time aside each day to pray. She commented that it may be difficult at first to keep to the commitment, "But after a while, it will seem like you've missed breakfast, if you skip a day."

I began to attend Mass three mornings a week, and adhered to a daily prayer routine. I'd sit in the chair beside my bed, turn off my phone, and set a timer for fifty minutes. I'd remind myself that I was in God's presence. That I was his son, one with Jesus before our Abba. I'd imagine that Claire was beside me. We were praying together. I used the scripture readings of the day's Mass as an aid.

I had no transformative experiences. No joy-filled moments. After I'd read the gospel of the day, it would often vanish from memory, like I'd never read it. Gradually, I began to pray, like a mantra, as perhaps Jesus had prayed, "Father, teach us to love." By "us" I meant, as Jesus would have meant, all of us.

IN MY INMOST BEING, YOU TEACH ME WISDOM

Everyone in the world. The timer would sound, and I was glad the prayer session was over. I'd thank God, and then ask God to help me pray the next time. Had I missed a day of prayer, I would have felt guilty—but I wouldn't have felt like I'd missed breakfast! But, as months and now years passed, I do feel something essential is missing if I omit the daily meditation.

I started to make conscious changes in how I lived each day. I started by saying "Yes" to all occasions. But now I was saying yes, not as a way of avoiding becoming a shut-in, but as a way of loving. I was beginning to say yes, because that is how I would like others to respond to my requests, and that is how, I believe, God responds to our requests.

I returned to the Abbey in April 2017, during Easter week, and again in late August. On the August visit I had a new awareness. I enjoy reading *The New York Review of Books* at lunch. I had forgotten to bring it, so I took a book from the guest book rack, Henri Nouwen's *A Sorrow Shared*, reflections on his mother's death and a letter of consolation to his father.[15]

Nouwen describes his mother's funeral as well as his time with his father, brother, and sister. Then he says, "Returning to the United States was returning to my grief." He writes about wanting to get back to a busy routine, but finds instead that he has a light calendar, extended periods of unscheduled time. Time during which he reflects on his mother's death, and the meaning of her struggle with death.

He ponders how "The disciples of Jesus (after Jesus' death) kept themselves isolated from the people for forty days, trying to comprehend what had happened. The long period of mourning was necessary before they were able to receive the Spirit."[16]

Then Nouwen writes, "If mother's agony and death were indeed an agony and death with Christ, should I not then hope that she would also participate in the sending of the Spirit? The deeper I entered my own grief, the more I became aware that something new was about to be born, something that I had not known before. I began to wonder if Jesus does not send his Spirit every time someone with whom we are connected by bonds of love leaves us. I started to feel the power of Jesus' words: 'It is for your own good that I am going because unless I go, the Advocate (the Spirit) will not come to you; but if I go, I will send him to you.'"[17]

I was struck by the thought that "something new was about to be born," and that Claire might participate with God in sending me the Holy Spirit.

The Psalm in the Mass the day after I returned from the Abbey read,

Where can I go from your spirit?
From your presence, where can I flee?
If I take the wings of the dawn,
If I settle at the farthest limits of the sea,
Even there your hand shall guide me,
And your right hand hold me fast.[18]

EPILOGUE

I was surprised to see that Claire, in her will, made a bequest to Saint Mary Star of the Sea elementary school, "in memory of Sr. Margaret Saint Paul Cawley, SND, my fifth-grade teacher." There were eight bequests in the will, to her brother John, to four nieces and a nephew (her brother John and sister-in-law Liz's children), to Jim McDonough, and to Sr. Margaret Saint Paul.

Saint Mary's is now The Saints Academy. I added to Claire's bequest and endowed an annual scholarship, *The Saints Academy Claire Lyons Callahan Scholarship Fund, in memory of Sr. Margaret Saint Paul Cawley.*

The first two scholarships were awarded in September 2017. In the summer of 2018, Daniel Bouchard, the Academy principal, asked if I would agree to be honored, with Claire (In Memoriam), by receiving the Academy's E Pluribus Unum Award at the annual Gala. I wanted to decline until he said, "It would help the Academy."

The event was at the Danvers Yacht Club in late November. Claire's home at 34 River St. was just across the water. I paused in the parking lot and gazed at it, tears welling in my eyes. To think that Claire had started out under such difficult circumstances, and gone on to live a life of love and service—it gave me hope for the children whose lives would be changed by the scholarships.

The reception area and large banquet room were decorated with brightly lit Christmas trees, red-bowed wreaths, and poinsettias. Tables-in-the-round were set with white table clothes, silver, and china. A brass-on-wood plaque was on display that described the scholarship; it included Sr. Margaret Saint Paul's and Claire's embossed photos and bios. A large video screen hung behind the elevated dais and speaker's rostrum. Before the presentation of each award, a video was played describing the award and showing photos of the recipients and family.

When Amy Burke asked what background music I wanted for our video collage, I said, "Let's use the Beatles' 'Let It Be.'" That is how Claire and I had tried to live the ups and downs of our lives. We tried to say, "Let it be" to the Spirit we knew was present in our lives.

In my remarks to the students' families and Academy supporters, I said I had come, not to be honored, but to honor them. To celebrate the love that caused them to put their own needs aside, so that they could afford to send their children to a private Catholic Academy where they would receive an excellent academic education, and learn how to love, learn especially what Christ meant when he said, "Love one another as I have loved you."

I told them how Sr. Margaret Saint Paul had touched something in Claire that made her want to live a life of love, a love that transformed her and me. "My wish," I said, "is that your daughters and sons, as they grow and mature, will live loving lives and be transformed by love."

ACKNOWLEDGMENTS

I once had the joy of spending four days with a close friend and her family. Showing me the family cemetery plot, she told me she wanted her headstone to read, "So Grateful."

Reflecting on that wonderful sentiment, I realized that, when I see God, I hope my first words will be "Thank you."[1]

This book took me seven years to write. It began as a dialogue with Claire, just weeks after her passing; an effort to hold on to Claire, to keep her present in my life.

That private dialogue evolved into a wish to keep Claire's memory alive in her family, to leave them a memoir of a woman they came to know well only in her late years, because she had lived her earlier years in other parts of the country.

But in telling Claire's story, I necessarily had to tell mine, because I was part of her life for fifty-one years.

In telling my life, I was reminded hundreds of times of how loved I have been. How privileged to be born in a country, and into a family where I have been nurtured and raised in the Catholic faith; and where I have been educated and have spent my adult life in service professions where colleagues welcomed me, and trusted my contributions and leadership.

In writing these acknowledgments, I want to thank not just those many who helped me write the memoir, but the many who, from my first breath until now, have helped instill in me the grateful heart that made me want to write it.

NOTES

Chapter 1

1. Zollo, R.P. *Danvers: The World Within Its Borders, Reflections on Its Diversity in the Twentieth Century*, Danvers, MA; p. 129.

Chapter 2

1. https://www.britannica.com/topic/Society-of-United-Irishmen; https://www.yourirish.com/history/18th-century/1796-the-french-attempt-to-aid-ireland (Visited: July 19, 2020).
2. The *Boston American* was a daily tabloid newspaper published in Boston, Massachusetts from March 21, 1904, until September 30, 1961. The newspaper was part of William Randolph Hearst's chain, and thus was also known as Hearst's Boston American. https://en.wikipedia.org/wiki/Boston_American (Visited: June 5, 2023).

Chapter 3

1. Matthew 5:10.

   Blessed are the poor in spirit,
   for theirs is the kingdom of heaven.

   Blessed are they who mourn,
   for they will be comforted.

   Blessed are the meek,
   for they will inherit the land.

*Blessed are they who hunger and thirst for righteousness,
for they will be satisfied.*

*Blessed are the merciful,
for they will be shown mercy.*

*Blessed are the clean in heart,
for they will see God.*

*Blessed are the peacemakers,
for they will be called children of God.*

*Blessed are they who are persecuted for the sake of righteousness,
for theirs is the kingdom of heaven.*

Chapter 4

1. https://www.aa.org/the-twelve-steps (Visited: April 19, 2023).

Chapter 6

1. https://www.washingtonpost.com/archive/local/1997/12/19/nicaraguan-diplomat-guillermo-sevilla-sacasa/df9e522f-0055-42ac-9a58-9c461c2465d9/ AND: https://en.wikipedia.org/wiki/Guillermo_Sevilla_Sacasa (Visited: March 26, 2023).

2. "Now a ritzy enclave known as Midtown West, from the 1930s through the 1960s Hell's Kitchen [was] anything but glamorous. Families lived hand-to-mouth; many teenagers dropped out of high school to work and help their parents make ends meet. https://www.aarp.org/politics-society/history/info-01-2008/true_west_side_stories.html (Visited: October 7, 2020).

"The changes in Hell's Kitchen and other West Side neighborhoods would amaze Jerome Robbins, who brought the 1957 musical "West Side Story" to the Broadway stage. The movie version won 10 Academy Awards."

https://www.fredericknewspost.com/news/lifestyle/travel_and_outdoors/west-side-story-hell-s-kitchen-has-become-one-of-new-york-city-s-most/article_d180aa55-6049-57a7-812c-727f3c5068c6.html (Visited: April 26, 2023).

3. General Arthur Farragut Twining had recently (1957) been appointed by President Eisenhower as chairman of the Joint Chiefs of Staff.

Five years later he would co-chair a Security Council special committee that published: *The ABM and the Changed Strategic Military Balance: A Study*. What more definitive expert source on the issue was there!

Chapter 7

1. *Dogmatic Constitution on the Church*, Chapter V: The Call of the Whole Church to Holiness. In Abbott, W.M. (General Editor), *The Documents of Vatican II*. New York: Guild Press, 1966, p. 67.

Chapter 8

1. Matlock, C.B. "She'll be off to Paris on Fulbright Grant." *Austin American Statesman*, April 11, 1965.
2. Koile, E. *Listening as a Way of Becoming*. Regency Books, a division of Word Books, Publisher. Waco, TX, 1977. *Your Secret Self*. Calibre, a division of Word Books, Publisher. Waco, TX, 1978.
3. Rogers, C.R. *Client-centered Therapy: Its Current Practice, Implications, and Theory*. Boston: Houghton Mifflin, 1951; *On Becoming a Person: A Therapist's View of Psychotherapy*. New York: Houghton Mifflin, 1961; *A Way of Being*. New York: Houghton Mifflin, 1980.
4. Matthew 22:38.

Chapter 9

1. May, A.R. *Crimetown U.S.A.: The History of the Mahoning Valley Mafia: Organized Crime Activity in Ohio's Steel Valley 1933-1963*, 2013. https://www.leanasbooks.com/book/9780983703754 (Visited: April 20, 2023).
2. Stassinopoulos, A. *Maria Callas: The Woman Behind the Legend*. New York: Simon & Schuster, 1981, p. 69.

Chapter 10

1. Alfaro, J.B. *Adnotationes in Tractatum De Virtutibus; Schemata Lectionum explicata a P. Joanne B. Alfaro, S.J.*, (ad usum privatum), Pontificia Universitas Gregoriana, Roma 1959; p. 3. (The English translation is my own.)
2. Ibid, pp. 10–11.
3. Aquinas. T. *Summa Theologiae* (1265–1274), IIa, IIae, q. xi, a.1.

Chapter 11

1. Matthew 15:21–28.
2. John 13:14.
3. Ayd, F.J., Jr. *Recognizing the Depressed Patient: With Essentials of Management and Treatment.* New York: Grune & Stratton, 1961.
4. https://acnp.org/about-us/ (Visited: April 20, 2023).
5. https://www.ncbi.nlm.nih.gov/pmc/articles/PMC2394633/ (Visited: April 20, 2023).
6. Mark 14:35–36.
7. Jesus' and St. Paul's Aramaic word that describes an intimate relationship (Papa, Daddy) with God our Father.
8. John 14:21.
9. Phil. 2:3.

Chapter 12

1. The Notre Dame Alumni office arranged an email correspondence between Drew and me. He had retired as Professor Emeritus from the University of Oklahoma College of Law where he specialized in agricultural law. We spoke by phone on December 21, 2020. I am grateful to Drew for the details of how Mike died, and for his comforting words to me.

Chapter 15

1. Revelation 22:13.

Chapter 16

1. Musa, M. *Dante's Vita Nuova: A Translation and an Essay.* Indiana University Press, 1973, p. 25.
2. *Catechism of the Catholic Church*, United States Catholic Conference, Inc. Libreria Editrice Vaticana; Mahwah, NJ: Paulist Press, 1994, p. 439 (1782).
3. *Pastoral Constitution on the Church in the Modern World (Gaudium et Spes)*, Chapter I, The Dignity of the Human Person, 16. In, Abbott, W.M. (general editor), *The Documents of Vatican II.* New York: Guild Press, 1966, pp. 213–214.

4. October 15, 1969. Letter from James F. Callahan to His Holiness, Pope Paul VI, Vatican City.

5. "It is true that someone validly ordained can, for a just reason, be discharged from the obligations and functions linked to ordination, or can be forbidden to exercise them; but he cannot become a layman again in the strict sense, because the character imprinted by ordination is forever. The vocation and mission received on the day of his ordination mark him permanently." *Catechism of the Catholic Church*, Part Two, Section Two, Chapter Three, Article 6. VII: 1583; *The Effects of the Sacrament of Holy Orders*. English translation for the United States of America, United States Catholic Conference, Inc., Libreria Editrice Vaticana. Mahwah, NJ: Paulist Press, 1994.

"Once validly received, sacred ordination never becomes invalid." *Code of Canon Law*, Latin/English Edition, Chapter IV: Loss of the Clerical State, Canon 290. Canon Law Society of America, Washington, D.C., 1983.

6. McGillicuddy, E.G. *Sing to Me and I Will Hear You: The Poems*. Thiensville, WI: Caritas Communications, 2012, p. 1.

Chapter 17

1. https://www.findagrave.com/memorial/95928348/walter-joseph-dalton (Visited: February 7, 2018).

2. Song of Songs 2:8–14.

3. Hofmann, Paul. Special to *The New York Times*, April 9, 1971. https://www.nytimes.com/1971/04/09/archives/pope-paul-compares-defecting-priests-to-judas.html (Visited: January 17, 2021). For an English translation of the pope's complete April 8, 1971 Holy Thursday homily, visit: https://www.vatican.va/content/paul-vi/it/homilies/1971/documents/hf_p-vi_hom_19710408.html (Visited: April 20, 2023).

Chapter 18

1. American Psychological Association definition: https://dictionary.apa.org/behavior-therapy) (Visited: March 31, 2023); Callahan, C.L. *Application of Selected Learning Principles to the Psychotherapeutic Treatment of a Hospitalized Patient: A Case Study of the Successful Treatment of a Severely Mentally Ill Patient*, a thesis written for a master's degree in counseling psychology, University of Texas at Austin, 1972.

2. For example, tokens could be earned for getting up on time (three tokens), bathing (three), exercising (four), and engaging in planned social behaviors (four).

3. Tokens could be "spent" positively or negatively. Examples of positive spending are watching TV (one token per hour), bowling at the hospital bowling alley (one token per game), and buying snacks at the hospital store (two tokens per snack).

Examples of negative spending (loss of tokens): non-attendance at group functions (five tokens), demands for medications that have not been prescribed, and are not appropriate for the patient's condition (four tokens), and verbal or physical assault on a fellow patient or member of the staff.

4. All the following text in quotation marks is from Claire's thesis. To lessen the distractions for the reader, I have not cited pages for each quotation.

5. Emily often spoke of burgle bars, but "could not explain what 'burgle bars' were, and I never did find out."

6. $527 in 2022.

Chapter 19

1. John 16:28.

Chapter 20

1. In his later career, Father D'Agostino went as a Jesuit missionary to Kenya where he opened one of the first orphanages for abandoned HIV-positive children. He died on November 20, 2006 of cardiac arrest at the Karen Hospital in Nairobi. To read an account of this remarkable man's life, see Holley, Joe. "Obituary, Rev. Angelo D'Agostino." *Washington Post*, November 22, 2006. https://www.washingtonpost.com/archive/local/2006/11/22/angelo-dagostino/f639fb9c-dc97-4695-ba91-18e32ff624bf/?utm_term=.77195231ea5a. (Visited: May 18, 2018).

Chapter 21

1. "Shillelaghs are clubs or Irish walking sticks crafted from the stout, knobby branches of trees which are shaped into a heavy 'hitting' end with varying lengths of handle. Blackthorn and oak, especially the root, are commonly used to craft shillelaghs." https://celticranch.com (Visited: April 3, 2023).

2. Brown, P. *Through the Eye of the Needle: Wealth, the Fall of Rome, and the Making of Christianity in the West, 350–550 AD*. Princeton University Press, 2012, p. 133; quoted in https://en.wikipedia.org/wiki/Ambrose (Visited: August 21, 2018).
3. John 13:12–15.

Chapter 22

1. "The *Monstrance* . . . is the vessel used in the Roman Catholic Church to exhibit objects of devotion, such as the Consecrated Eucharistic Host during Eucharistic Adoration or Benediction of the Blessed Sacrament. The word *Monstrance* comes from the Latin word *monstrare* meaning 'to show.'" https://www.catholicdoors.com/faq/1500/qu1570.htm (Visited: April 4, 2023).
2. Micah: 6:6, 8–9.
3. Copy of Claire's letter to Fr. Keyes for Phil's homily (found in Claire's files).
4. https://www.wunderground.com/history/daily/us/ma/boston/KBOS/date/1991-8-19 (Visited: February 5, 2021).
5. https://www.washingtonpost.com/archive/local/1993/11/02/obituaries/80450b69-2a71-4afc-967e-2c661303fd80/ (Visited: April 23, 2023).

Chapter 23

1. https://www.cancer.net/cancer-types/liver-cancer/statistics#:~:text=For%20the%2043%25%20of%20people,relative%20survival%20rate%20is%2013%25. (Visited: April 20, 2023).

Chapter 24

1. "Sed rate, or erythrocyte sedimentation rate (ESR), is a blood test that can reveal inflammatory activity in your body." https://www.mayoclinic.org/tests-procedures/sed-rate/about/pac-20384797 (Visited: September 27, 2021).
2. "Giant cell arteritis is an inflammation of the lining of arteries, most often, the temporal arteries. For this reason, it is sometimes called temporal arteritis. The lining of the arteries becomes inflamed, causing them to swell. This narrows the blood vessels, reducing the amount of blood, oxygen and vital nutrients to reach the body's tissues."

The cause of giant cell arteritis is unknown. It usually occurs between ages seventy to eighty. Women are twice as likely than men to develop the disease, and it is more common among whites of northern European or Scandinavian descent. And about 50 percent of people with giant cell arteritis have polymyalgia rheumatica. http://www.mayoclinic.org/diseases-conditions/giant-cell-arteritis/basics/definition/con-20023109 (Visited: June 3, 2021).

3. "Polymyalgia rheumatica is an infrequently occurring, inflammatory condition that causes pain or aching in the large muscle groups, especially around the shoulders and hips. Polymyalgia literally means 'pain in many muscles.' Rheumatica means 'changing' or 'in flux.' https://www.webmd.com/arthritis/polymyalgia-rheumatica-temporal-arteritis (Visited: June 3, 2021).

4. Anonymous Greek poet.

Chapter 25

1. https://www.votf.org/about/ (Visited: April 20, 2023).

Chapter 26

1. C-Span-2 In Depth. Interview with Cornel West, Ph.D. For more on Cornel West: https://en.wikipedia.org/wiki/Cornel_West (Visited: April 17, 2021).

2. Romans 8:18.

Chapter 27

1. Musa, Mark. *Dante's Vita Nuova: A Translation and an Essay* (A new edition). Chapter XXXI: Canzone (L'occhi dolente per pieta del core), stanza four. Indiana University Press, 1973; p. 65.

2. Lewis, C.S., *A Grief Observed*. New York: Bantam Books, 1976, pp. 28–29. (Originally published 1963 by Faber & Faber, London).

3. Didion, Joan. *The Year of Magical Thinking*. New York: Alfred A. Knopf, 2005.

4. Saint Augustine (Bishop of Hippo). *The Confessions*, translated by Maria Boulding, O.S.B, Vintage Spiritual Classics. New York: Vintage Books, 1998, p. 222.

Chapter 28

1. In 2012, Dr. Kevin Kunz became the ABAM EVP. With remarkable dedication, skill, and genius he worked with the ABAM board, the White House, the National Institutes of Health, and the leaders of medical specialties and health care systems to demonstrate that it was time to recognize addiction medicine, and permit all physicians to apply to be certified. Addiction Medicine was recognized in October 2015. The first requirement of a new medical specialty is to establish fellowship training programs for physicians in the nation's medical centers.
2. Dunne. J.S. *A Journey with God in Time: A Spiritual Quest.* University of Notre Dame Press, 2003, p. 10.
3. Ibid., p. 75.
4. Ibid., p. 72.
5. Ibid., p. 39.
6. Ibid., p. 140. These are "four little sentences" that Dunne "took to be four spiritual truths." These sentences, he says, are "scattered through the story of J.R.R. Tolkien's *The Lord of the Rings.*"
7. http://mixerrreviews.blogspot.com/2017/06/history-of-travis-state-school-revisited.html (Visited: April 27, 2021).
8. https://www.findagrave.com/cemetery/2212565/travis-state-school-cemetery#view-photo=78640194 (Visited: April 20, 2023).
9. http://www.liturgies.net/Liturgies/Catholic/roman_missal/prefaces.htm#dead2 (Visited: April 24, 2021).
10. 1 Cor. 13:8.
11. 1 Cor. 13:13.
12. 1 Cor. 14:1.
13. 1 John 4:8.
14. https://msmabbey.org/ (Visited: April 20, 2023).
15. Nouwen, H.J.M. *A Sorrow Shared.* Ave Maria Press, 2010.
16. Ibid., pp. 43–44.
17. Ibid. p. 44. John 14:17.
18. Ps. 139:7–10.

Acknowledgments

1. "Beloved, we are God's children now; what we will be has not yet been revealed. What we do know is this: When he is revealed, we will be like him, for we will see him as he is." (1 John 3:2).

www.ingramcontent.com/pod-product-compliance
Lightning Source LLC
Chambersburg PA
CBHW060523080526
44586CB00012B/583